# Black Wall Street and the Tulsa Race M
## Destruction of America's Wealthiest Afric

### By Charles River Editors

# About Charles River Editors

**Charles River Editors** is a boutique digital publishing company, specializing in bringing history back to life with educational and engaging books on a wide range of topics. Keep up to date with our new and free offerings with this 5 second sign up on our weekly mailing list, and visit Our Kindle Author Page to see other recently published Kindle titles.

We make these books for you and always want to know our readers' opinions, so we encourage you to leave reviews and look forward to publishing new and exciting titles each week.

# Introduction

In the wake of the Civil War, African Americans attained freedom from chattel slavery, but continued to suffer discrimination both legal in the form of Jim Crow laws and de facto in the continued perception among the vast majority of white Americans that African Americans were at the very least inferior and at the most a constant dangerous presence in their communities who must be carefully controlled. In this way, Tulsa was no different than most cities in the region in the 1920s.

Overall, Tulsa in 1921 was considered a modern, vibrant city. What had fueled this remarkable growth was oil, specifically the discovery of the Glenn Pool oil field in 1905. Within five years, Tulsa had grown from a rural crossroads town in the former Indian Territory into a boomtown with more than 10,000 citizens, and as word spread of the fortunes that could be made in Tulsa, people of all races poured into the city. By 1920, the greater Tulsa area boasted a population of over 100,000. In turn, Tulsa's residential neighborhoods were some of the most modern and stylish in the country, and the Tulsa Chamber of Commerce produced postcards and literature boasting of the virtues of life in their modern oil city. However, as a commission report about the Tulsa Riot later pointed out, "What the pamphlets and the picture postcards did not reveal was that, despite of its impressive new architecture and its increasingly urbane affectations, Tulsa was a deeply troubled town. As 1920 turned into 1921, the city would soon face a crossroads that, in the end, would change it forever...Tulsa was, in some ways, not one city but two."

When they came to Tulsa, many blacks settled in the Greenwood area and established a thriving commercial, cultural, and residential area. Of course, the segregation was forced on these residents, and while they had fled the worst conditions of the Jim Crow South in other areas, they were not able to escape it completely. But in one way, Tulsa was different for African Americans, as black citizens of the city shared in the city's wealth, albeit not as equally as their white neighbors. The Greenwood district, a 36 square block section of northern Tulsa, was considered the wealthiest African American neighborhood in the country, called the "Black Wall Street" because of the large number of affluent and professional residents. In the 2001 final report of the Oklahoma Commission to Study the Tulsa Race Riot of 1921, historians John Hope Franklin and Scott Ellsworth described the Greenwood area that would be all but destroyed in one of America's most notorious riots: "In less than twenty-four hours, nearly all of Tulsa's African-American residential district--some forty-square-blocks in all--had been laid to waste, leaving nearly nine-thousand people homeless. Gone, too, was the city's African American commercial district, a thriving area located among Greenwood Avenue which boasted some of the finest black-owned businesses in the Southwest. The Stradford Hotel, a modern fifty-four room brick establishment which housed a drug store, barber shop, restaurant and banquet hall, had been burned to the ground. So had the Gurley Hotel, the Red Wing Hotel, and the Midway Hotel. Literally dozens of family-run businesses--from cafes and mom-and-pop grocery stores, to the Dreamland Theater, the Y.M.C.A. cleaners, the East End Feed Store, and Osborne Monroe's roller skating rink--had also gone up in flames, taking with them the livelihoods, and in many cases the life savings, of literally hundreds of people. The offices of two newspapers--the *Tulsa Star* and the *Oklahoma Sun*-- had also been destroyed, as were the offices of more than a dozen doctors, dentists, lawyers, realtors, and other professionals. A United States Post Office substation was burned as was the all-black Frissell Memorial Hospital. The brand new Booker T. Washington High School building escaped the torches of the rioters, but Dunbar Elementary School did not. Neither did more than a half dozen African-American churches, including the newly constructed Mount Zion Baptist Church, an impressive brick tabernacle which had been dedicated only seven weeks earlier."

The death knell for Black Wall Street began on Memorial Day, May 31, 1921. Around or after 4:00 p.m. that day, a clerk at Renberg's clothing store on the first floor of the Drexel Building in Tulsa heard a woman scream. Turning in the direction of the scream, he saw a young black man running from the building. Going to the elevator, the clerk found the white elevator operator, 17-year-old Sarah Page, crying and distraught. The clerk concluded that she had been assaulted by the black man he saw running a few moments earlier and called the police.

Those facts are just about the only things people agree on when it comes to the riot in Tulsa in 1921. By the time the unrest ended, an unknown number of Tulsa's black citizens were dead, over 800 people were injured, and what had been the wealthiest black community in the United States had been laid to waste.

In the days after the riot, a group formed to work on rebuilding the Greenwood neighborhood, which had been all but destroyed. The former mayor of Tulsa, Judge J. Martin, declared, "Tulsa can only redeem herself from the country-wide shame and humiliation into which she is today plunged by complete restitution and rehabilitation of the destroyed black belt. The rest of the

United States must know that the real citizenship of Tulsa weeps at this unspeakable crime and will make good the damage, so far as it can be done, to the last penny."

However, financial assistance would be slow in coming, a jury would find that black mobs were responsible for the damage, and not a single person was ever convicted as a result of the riot. Indeed, given that racist violence directed at blacks was the norm in the Jim Crow South, and accusations of black teens or adults violating young white girls were often accepted without evidence, people barely batted an eye at the damage wrought by the riot. Tragically, the decades following the riot saw the memory of it recede into the background. The *Tulsa Tribune* did not recognize the riot in its "Fifteen Years Ago Today" or "Twenty-five Years Ago Today" features. In 1971, the Tulsa Chamber of Commerce decided to commemorate the riot, but when they read the materials gathered by Ed Wheeler about the riot, they refused to publish any of it, and the Tulsa papers also refused to run Wheeler's story. He finally published an article in a black magazine, *Impact Magazine*; but most of Tulsa's white citizens never knew about it. It would not be until recently that a true accounting of the riot and its damage have been conducted, and as the 100th anniversary of the massacre approaches in 2021, the city of Tulsa is still working to complete the historical record.

*Black Wall Street and the Tulsa Race Massacre: The Creation and Destruction of America's Wealthiest African American Neighborhood* chronicles the rise and fall of the Greenwood District. Along with pictures depicting important people, places, and events, you will learn about Black Wall Street and the Tulsa Race Massacre like never before.

Black Wall Street and the Tulsa Race Massacre: The Creation and Destruction of America's Wealthiest African American Neighborhood

## Before the Rise of Black Wall Street

The historical quest for economic prosperity among non-white cultures in the United States was dealt a nearly unplayable hand from the country's founding. African Americans, who built much of the nation's infrastructure through its first century of existence, had no ancestral access to western wealth, lived under a status scarcely above that ascribed to beasts of burden, and found few champions outside their own culture. A stolen and enslaved people, efforts to demonstrate equal intelligence, worthiness of education, aspirations toward tangible success, and the drive to prosper was counterproductive to a white system dependent on their continued subjugation.

The "emancipation" granted by Lincoln's Emancipation Proclamation signaled a technical status of freedom for the slave, but it did not in any sense guarantee social equality. After all, such a status lies beyond the power of legislation if the dominant culture would not tolerate or otherwise embrace the idea. Every pursuit of employment began with a racial disadvantage, and the Jim Crow laws in the South effectively reinstated a constraint on much of the slaves' range of movement, opportunity, and right to civic participation.

By the approach of the 20th century two strategies had come to the forefront for black advancement. Booker T. Washington envisioned a rise in his culture's former slave status by developing a general usefulness in what would now be known as blue-collar labor or basic agricultural skills. However, for W.E.B. Du Bois, the underlying equation of subservience was unaltered as his race moved from slave labor to poorly paid lackeys at the lowest levels of white business. Du Bois exhorted the African American to stand and declare his right to prosperity, education, and status within an economic system predisposed to shutting him out. Either way, positions of leadership and the time of middle and upper-tier wage earning was far off. However, in a phenomenon scantily taught in secondary education of the twenty-first century, African America gained its footing with a third approach that in developmental terms combined the Washington and Du Bois models.

**Washington**

**Du Bois**

The alteration from a standard habit of begging or demanding status from a race for which equality was counterproductive was to be found in cultural and physical isolation, entrepreneurship, self-help and internally generated profit. Black business interests managed to rid themselves of white hierarchy in a few spots on the east coast and in the Midwest. Land was bought and sold exclusively within the black community, and the currency generated remained in the black system. All kinds of businesses were established in mono-racial enclaves with assistance from black lending institutions devoted to increased opportunity for African American success.

The most notable example of these black *Camelots* - organized, efficient, wealthy and collaborative - rose out of the city of Tulsa, Oklahoma on hostile ground where the black man occupied the lowest rung of civil rights. Hundreds of businesses ranging from the essential to the luxurious effectively debunked white stereotypes of African American laziness, mental deficiency, immorality, and general shiftlessness. White Tulsans looked on while their neighbors, the children of slaves, met or outpaced their standard of living. A culture that was once forbidden to receive basic literacy now sent their children to institutions such as Columbia University, Tuskegee Institute under the guidance of Washington, Howard University, and Spelman College.

Indeed, what was to become hailed as "Black Wall Street" in the enclave of the Greenwood District led the region in high-level financing and demonstrated sophisticated investment skills that outpaced the city norm. The school system became a model of success, and residents bought fine homes, maintained an opulent social life, and became patrons of the arts. Naturally, former slaves had always desired access to the same opportunities and possessions of their masters, along with the freedom to employ them at will. The secret seemed to be found in constructive segregation, living apart and asking nothing from a resentful outside world whose objective it was to leave the black community in debt.

The Greenwood District of Tulsa was not the only example of socioeconomic triumph created by the first generation that followed emancipation. The Jackson Ward of Richmond, Virginia became the "epicenter of black banking"[1] in the otherwise rigid environment of Jim Crow prevalent in other sections of the city. Hayti, North Carolina, named for the Caribbean island nation of Haiti, prospered amidst the population of Durham. Freedmen had come to work in the tobacco warehouses, and in time created North Carolina Life Insurance, the wealthiest black-owned company in the state. The administrators added all manner of land development, including a self-sufficient hospital staffed with black doctors and nurses. By the first decade of the 20th century, a library, theater, and 200 retail businesses had been added. Similar examples could be found in the "Little Harlem" of Birmingham, Alabama, Marcus Garvey's Harlem in New York City, and in the following decades, Boley, Oklahoma.

The establishment of black prosperity in Tulsa came about as the culmination of several factors, the first being the destruction of the American South. Both the land and aristocratic life within the plantation culture were shattered, and with a sporadic industrial capacity, recovery proceeded at a snail's pace. The post-civil war years comprised an era of migrations, from Native American relocations to blacks seeking escape from Jim Crow. Lincoln could speak all he liked of emancipation, but he could not alter the caste system of the South. The white overlord was determined to retain his liberated black labor force under an alternate set of legal restraints.

The great bulk of the American South, barren and unproductive after the sweeping Union invasions, was unkind to the farmers above all others.. Eking out a bare existence for black sharecroppers left them constantly on the borders of bankruptcy and starvation. In order to approximate the pre-war status of slaves and to keep in place old traditions of behavior and financial struggle among the newly emancipated, the Democratic Party established Jim Crow to sustain white supremacy in the region. The concept consisted of a tangle of state and local statutes controlling black behavior, named after a minstrel show character of the time, and these extreme legislations endured for decades, keeping black America legally subjugated past the mid-20th century. Jim Crow maintained a state of segregation, suppressed the rights of non-whites to vote, barred access to a formal education, and set a strict code of public behavior. To understand the code was paramount, and violating it was perilous to one's safety. Black residents

---

[1] Michael Harriot, The Other Black Wall Streets, The Root – www.theroot.com, the-other-black-wall-streets-1823010812

could not go certain places in white communities, could not freely seek employment above their station, and could not bargain freely for wages. Blacks in financial arrears were attached to families as indentured servants, and children of any age could be seized for labor or collateral. The code was not only instituted to maintain dominance over black residents, but for the poor of any color.

The code was overseen by former Confederate soldiers who took up positions as post-war police officers, judges, and politicians, and behind the entire phenomenon loomed the Ku Klux Klan, a terrorist group keeping non-whites in line through acts of violence and intimidation. The KKK was established at the war's end in Pulaski, Tennessee as a private club for former Confederate officers. Some suggest that the "white hood brigade"[2] was initiated by Confederate General Nathan Bedford Forrest, who viewed blacks as human beings rather than statistics and "troublemakers."[3] Forrest apparently severed his association with the first chapter after "undesirables"[4] perverted the group's ideals.

According to Glenda Gilmore of Yale University, the stranglehold Jim Crow exerted on the South was malleable as black residents and white sympathizers explored new methods of resistance, requiring the system to "prove its power"[5] on a regular basis. The code was forced to rebrand and re-legislate itself as politicians struggled to retain their grip. With enough support from outside the black population, its power was never "complete or total." Thus, in the end, the Southern black sharecroppers who were financially clear of servitude but bound to a marginal existence held one ace – to pack what little they had and leave for better places with less abusive histories.

As a result, even as freedom from slavery represented a "radical transformation"[6] for the African American population, despite the change in technical and legal status as citizens, the economic and demographic realities were not so significantly altered. According to the 1890 Census, 90% of blacks still lived in the South, roughly the same percentage as 20 years prior. Three quarters of the black population was located in rural areas, and less than one half owned their own home. Whites owned their homes at twice that rate, and half of all black men and 35% of black women were either farmers or farm laborers, a vastly higher percentage than that of the white population. African Americans were largely consigned to unskilled positions, and the percentage of children attending school was far lower than it was for white families. The style of life for blacks was largely a continuation of the past century, taken up with cotton agriculture.

---

[2] Jerry Bowyer, Tulsa Massacre: The Loser Class vs. Black Entrepreneurs, Townhall Finance, June 23, 2020 – www.finance.townhall.com/columnists/jerrybowyer/2020/06/23/tulsa-massacre-the-loser-class-vs-black-entrepreneurs-n2571165

[3]Oklahoma Historical Society, Ku Klux Klan-www.okhistory.org/publications/enc/entry.php?entry=KU001

[4] Oklahoma Historical Society

[5] Glenda Gilmore, Jumpin' Jim Crow: Southern Politics from Civil War to Civil Rights, Department of African American Studies, Yale University – www.afamstudies.yale.edu/publications/jumpin'-him-crow-Southern-politics-civil-war-civil-rights

[6] Thomas N. Maloney, University of Utah, African Americans in the 20th Century, E.H. Net – www.eh.net/encyclopedia/African Americans-in-the-20th-century

Some were part-time laborers while others worked as tenant farmers, renting the land and tools out of an already meager income. Wages between whites and blacks were similar for agricultural work, but white workers were far more likely to own land. They continued to hold higher-skill jobs, while blacks generally worked for lower-wage companies.

In conjunction, the laws against personal rights grew more severe than in the years prior to the Civil War. The Supreme Court's decision in *Plessy v. Ferguson* gave way to an ever-increasing state of segregation and allowed for separate facilities and services between the races. "Separate but equal" was the proposition sold to the black community, which was interesting and paradoxical since black-ordered segregation was to become the bedrock of financial success. Jim Crow laws segregated the schools, all manner of public transportation, lodgings, and government buildings. The accompanying requirement for equal treatment in this divided society was seldom enforced. As an example, money was regularly diverted from the black school systems and funneled into white schools. White teacher salaries rose on a per-pupil basis, while black schools fell into a sharp decline.

By the second decade of the 20th century, the South was altered by a massive northward migration of black workers, causing a four percent drop in the black population over the period of just a few years. The northward movement was in every way tied to either economic circumstances and/or fear of the KKK. Many Northern employers in several industries were experiencing an increased demand for their products and thus required a larger and immediate labor force. The traditional source of labor, immigrants from Europe, dried up due to World War I, while the international flow of immigrant workers was interrupted and worsened by the passage of harsher anti-immigration laws. Turning to African American labor, employers sent recruiters into the South, raising the prospect of a higher wage than the Southern employers could provide and offering to pay each man's way to the factory's location. The North also looked all the better as the boll weevil and weather abnormalities wreaked havoc with the cotton crop. Although black America did not rise out of the unskilled category, the pay was significantly better, and the fields of opportunity were vastly broader.

Of course, there were drawbacks to moving north. Admittance to certain firms could not be procured by black citizens, especially new Southern arrivals. The Ford Motor Company hired many, but other major automakers in Detroit would not, and in many cases, blacks took on unpleasant and dangerous tasks shunned by some white workers. These included work in meat packing plants, foundry departments of auto companies, and blast furnaces in the production of steel. As unions gained strength in the North, their relationship with the new black workers was often "antagonistic."[7] Most passed explicit rules barring entry to black laborers. When faced with strikes, employers frequently hired black workers as strike-breakers. Black females found the pursuit of work a more difficult proposition as competition grew increasingly "heated"[8] among

[7] Thomas N. Maloney
[8] Oklahoma Historical Society

domestic workers.

**Tulsa**

Among the possible areas where a higher quality lifestyle was possible, the Oklahoma Territory ended up being a prime arrival point for those who chose to move west instead of north. Created only a year after the war's end, the pursuit of Oklahoma land came about through a request to the federal government to reduce Cheyenne, Comanche, and Arapaho lands, and once accomplished, the region was prepared for a land "rush," in which both whites and blacks were eligible for the pursuit of new acreage. The availability of land in the Oklahoma Territory was made possible by an earlier forced migration of Native Americans from the states of Georgia, Tennessee, Alabama, North Carolina, and Florida. Three decades before the Civil War, Andrew Jackson established the *Indian Removal Act* and sent native landowners on a forced march of 5,043 miles that wound through nine states, now referred to as the "Trail of Tears." Those thrown off their land walked the distance in double file, "many bound in chains."[9] Thousands died reaching what the government called the "Indian colonization zone" at the western edge of the Midwest.

For purposes of eventual statehood, native land was in perpetuity easy to redraw or reduce, depending on the perceived need, and people took advantage of the confiscated lands from the relocation. However, the generally unknown reality of the Trail of Tears is that the "Five Civilized Tribes," including the Cherokee, Choctaw, Chickasaw, Creek, and Seminole, brought their own black slaves on the forced march, and some of them went on to become crucial in the development of the Greenwood District. A number of the native leaders had acquired extraordinary wealth before taking the journey, such as half Scottish Chief John Ross, leader of the Cherokee Nation. Other wealthy colleagues joined him. A modern perception that one American president put the entire incident into motion is incorrect. The idea of native relocation spanned the administration of nine presidents, and removing them from the South and East was a "popularly endorsed, congressionally sanctioned"[10] scheme. Many speculated that in time, black slaves and their native masters would unite against white domination, but that never occurred. Among those who accompanied natives, most blacks were taken captive as stolen slaves, but there were a small number of freedmen, and a few hundred ran away from their Southern masters and sought haven with the tribes once having arrived in Oklahoma. They were welcomed at first as free people and often adopted as family members, but in time the tribes began purchasing them from the standard American slave markets. , and the Five Civilized Tribes were "deeply committed"[11] to slavery. Before the Civil War, blacks had already joined the tribe in numbers, and the Cherokee brought 1,500 to Oklahoma. The Creek Nation included 300 blacks, and

[9] History.com, The Trail of Tears, Feb. 21, 2020 – www.history.com/topics/native-american-history/trail-of-tears

[10] Ryan P. Smith how Native American Slaveholders Complicate the Trail of Tears Narrative, Smithsonian Magazine –
www.smithsonianmag.com/Smithsonian-institution/how-native-american-slaveholders-complicate-the-trail-of-tears-narrative

[11] Ryan P. Smith

approximately 1,200 were owned by the Chickasaw. Eventually, 8,000 black people were present among the tribes, and throughout this time, native leaders participated in a global economy driven by cotton. They believed without hesitation that they were equal to whites and superior to blacks.

The slaves who eventually reached the Greenwood District as citizens arrived through various diplomatic avenues, and rules governing slavery differed from tribe to tribe. As larger numbers of black refugees from the South arrived, the equation changed. Eventually, the Five Civilized Tribes were forced to accept land allotments in order to remain legal residents of the new state, and while the Dawes Act finalized federal control over Indian land, in a real sense the Native American population transported with their black slaves were the true founders of the city of Tulsa. Unlike emancipated slaves, tribal members were allowed to "own land, vote, and serve on juries"[12] in local judicial systems. After proving their "civility" to the federal government, they were allowed to participate in the social life of a nation that had once counted them as the statistical fraction of a human being regarding public transactions and legislative agendas.

Initially, Southern blacks saw the area as a possibility for the creation of towns and colonies in which they could experience their political rights without interference from Southern oppression. They were enticed to the region by figures such as Edwin McCabe, once the most powerful black man in Kansas. A politician and businessman, McCabe was largely responsible for the black settlement of the Oklahoma Territory. Born in Troy, New York, he served as a clerk on Wall Street before settling in the black town of Nicodemus, Kansas. Making his mark as an attorney, he ran successfully as the Republican candidate for State Auditor. As a speculator, he realized that Oklahoma could serve as a "haven from racism"[13] and be personally profitable. McCabe arrived at the future site of Langston, Oklahoma, a decade before the turn of the century, and established the *Langston City Herald*. The smaller enterprise was to serve as a prototype for the model that reached its culmination in Greenwood. Owning the bulk of available lots, his advertisements in the *Herald* declared the region to be "the paradise of Eden and the garden of the Gods."[14] He added a special draw for Southern blacks suffering under segregation and lynch laws. The advertisement read, "Here the negro can rest from mob law, here he can be secure from every ill of the Southern policies."[15]

These offers of land were strewn through Kansas, Arkansas, Texas, Louisiana, Missouri, and Tennessee, and by 1891, 200 Southern refugees lived in Langston City, including a doctor, minister, and schoolteacher. Soon after, thousands of African Americans arrived in time to participate in the "rush" for land, a brutal race employing whatever mode of transportation one could find. Most were ready to secure a home for themselves and their families "at any price."[16]

---

[12] Alaina E. Roberts, Assistant Professor, University of Pittsburgh, Commemorating the Tulsa Massacre: A Search for Identity and Historical Complexity, June 4, 2020 – www.ncph.org/history-at-work/commemorating-tulsa-massacre/

[13] Black Past, Edward P. McCabe (1850-1920) – www.blackpast.org/African American-history/maccabe-edwin-p-1850-1920/

[14] Immotionaaame.org

[15] Immotionaame.org

Racing through former Native American lands, they staked claims of 1.5 million acres in the Cherokee Strip, valued at $11 million in modern currency. By the start of the 1910s, the farming land had lost its crop price value, and many of the new residents were drawn to the cities.

E. P. M<sup>c</sup>CABE.

### McCabe

After purchasing 320 acres himself, McCabe nearly singlehandedly established the new town, naming it for a recently elected black Congressman. He hoped that the number of black settlers would in time propel him into the governor's office by the time of statehood. However, these dreams fell short when the new state adopted Jim Crow statutes and segregated public transportation. McCabe sold his house to fight the new laws, but the U.S. Supreme Court upheld the state's legislature. He died a deeply disappointed and relatively impoverished man in Chicago during the peak of the coming financial empire in the Greenwood District of Tulsa.

All in all, during the bulk of the great migration from the South, approximately 6 million African Americans relocated. They were pushed even harder by the Ku Klux Klan, despite the fact the KKK had been officially dissolved only four years after the war. Klan members continued to operate underground with the same effectiveness to which they had become

[16] Immotionaame.org

accustomed. Despite the terror perpetrated against blacks, the migration dismayed residents of the South. First, they had lost the war despite recapturing the services of its black citizens. Then, they lost the labor force that farmed their fields and built the bulk of their infrastructure.

The African American migration from the farmland produced a total of 32 all-black communities, of which Boley was the most active. Founded by two white entrepreneurs who hired a black man named Tom Haynes to promote the venture, Boley became an even more advanced financial model for the region. In 1905, Booker T. Washington visited and wrote glowingly of the breakthroughs he witnessed, all created by former Southern sharecroppers.

In 1907, Oklahoma achieved statehood. For the white population, the entrance into the union was a boon, but far less so for the black newcomers. The political makeup differed greatly from the modern day. The Republican Party was the liberal force in the expanding U.S., while the Democratic Party housed the Southern plantation families and Jim Crow devotees, and the latter won out in mapping the political fortunes of the new state. New legislation "quickly disenfranchised"[17] black voters and segregated the state school systems along with various other accommodations, creating a resemblance to Southern conditions.

Much of the impetus behind the rigid legislation came from notorious white supremacist Bill "Alfalfa" Murray. In his colorful career, he ran for many state and national offices, with a term as governor and Congressman, adding a later run for President. A Texan, his nickname came from a propensity to promote alfalfa as a crop. Unable to speak publicly without racial slurs, he was considered "something of a clown,"[18] but unfortunately for African Americans of the state, his message of racial warfare was timely, in step with the white voting base of his time. Soon, Jim Crow was as much a part of Oklahoma society as it had been in the Deep South, and the Klan, as it had elsewhere, also arrived.

---

[17] Immotionaame.org

[18] William W. Savage, Jr., History is Clear: Alfalfa Bill Murray was a Terrible Bigot, Thursday, June 18, 2020, Non Doc.com – www.nondoc.com/2020/06/18/alfalfa-bill-murray-was-a-terrible-bigot/

**Murray**

Some of the newcomers lost heart and went elsewhere, "disillusioned."[19] A fair-sized group went further north into Alberta, Canada. Others joined the "Back to Africa"[20] movement. A few hundred even joined the ill-fated Chief Sam expedition. Alfred C. "Chief" Sam, a self-declared African chief, purchased an aging freighter, sold berths, and took a boatload of returnees to Africa. They suffered investigations, deprivation, and were rerouted. Only a few reached Ghana to be warmly welcomed. Others dispersed to varied outcomes, and a second wave of passengers lost all they had when Sam sold the ship, stranding hundreds. Still others went south to Mexico.

All the while, racism limited the growth of some towns, as white residents signed oaths never to "rent, sell, or lease land within Okfuskee County to any person of Negro blood."[21] Thus, as

[19] Oklahoma Historical Society, All-Black Town – www.oklahomahistory.org/publications/end/entry-php?entry=AL009
[20] Oklahoma Historical Society
[21] Oklahoma Historical Society

local blacks departed, they left behind a withered tax base putting the towns in financial jeopardy. However, such was not the case in the Greenwood District of Tulsa, where several financial stars came together in an atmosphere of mutual assistance to create the best of the all-black cultures in the Oklahoma region. Already a wealthy area from the discovery of oil, the Greenwood District made sure that they would be included in the feast by controlling their own money in every step of the process.

According to the City Directory of Tulsa, 126 oil companies were operational in and around the city by the first years of the 20th century, and in the following decade, 11,000 black Tulsans would come to reside in the area. Not all of the oil barons who raised Tulsa from the prairie were white. For example, Jake Simmons, Jr. became the leading black entrepreneur in the entire oil industry despite his relatively late arrival in Greenwood. Among the recent immigrants of lesser wealth who came before, many were from Missouri. A large number of freedmen had for years lived in the region, many with the Five Civilized Tribes. As the most illustrious of all the midwestern black enclaves, the Greenwood District lived up to the promise inherent in McCabe's efforts in Langston. Established in the year before official Oklahoma statehood, the "venerable"[22] enclave soon housed a population of 10,000 and served as the most active and affluent entity of African American business and culture in the nation. The single street around which the entire enterprise functioned was Greenwood Avenue, in particular where it intersected with Archer Street.

[22] Alexis Clark, Tulsa's "Black Wall Street" Flourished as a Self-Contained Hub in Early 1900s, History.com – www.history.com/news/black-wall-street-tulsa-race-massacre

Interestingly enough, the broad central avenue was the only major thoroughfare that did not cross the tracks into virtually all-white Tulsa, and the intersection of Greenwood and Archer housed the headquarters of the project. Occupying and developing a larger share of Native American land, some of the black residents transferred from native ownership, while the tribes followed a varied set of rules governing the circumstances under which servants could be released.

What some called "Deep Greenwood,"[23] created by a disciplined organizational process while paralleling rapid population expansion, left "a minimum of order in its wake."[24] Corrupt practices on the part of police, as well as political and physical assaults by oilmen against the interests of their competitors, complicated the process, although the danger was somewhat minimized through insular living. Vigilante groups such as the Knights of Liberty wreaked havoc with the Greenwood contingent of International Workers of the World, an international labor union associated with socialism and anarchism. Communist movements have historically sought to turn black populations against societies that once enslaved them, and the Knights of Liberty likely feared that the black population of Greenwood, savvy as it was in the practice of capitalism, may be influenced as such. In the infamous "Tulsa Outrage," a district judge handed over 17 IWW workers to the Knights. They were driven to a desolate location west of town and held at gunpoint. Each victim was bound to a tree, tortured, then tarred and feathered. Their clothes were burned.

Throughout this time, Greenwood continued in its profitable way. Black prairie towns popped up after the Dawes Act allowed the federal government to partition the acreage owned by natives into individual plots, anathema to many tribal members of nomadic and far-ranging populations. However, only those who accepted the partitions were allowed citizenship, and over 90 million acres of tribal land were stripped from the original recipients in the end, given instead to non-natives, both white and black. Black purchasers were eager to amass real estate, and and the Greenwood District of Tulsa became the premiere example of it. Nowhere else had "so many African American men and women come together to create, occupy, and govern their own communities."[25] So heady was the experience that some envisioned a widespread black political bloc, while others imagined a black state in the heart of America.

### The Rise of Black Wall Street

Among the dynamic figures who created the Greenwood District's 35 square blocks was Ottawa W. Gurley, a wealthy landowner from the Deep South. Born in Huntsville, Alabama to

---

[23] Thomas F. Armstrong, Review of Scott Ellsworth's Death in a Promised Land, the Tulsa Race Riot of 1921, *Reviews in American History* Vol. 11 no. 1 (March1983) Johns Hopkins University Press

[24] Thomas F. Armstrong

[25] Oklahoma Historical Society

freed slaves, he grew up in Pine Bluff, Arkansas. Largely self-educated, he married childhood sweetheart Emma, a teacher. Gurley was serving in a "cushy" position with the federal Postal Service during the Grover Cleveland administration, but resigned to participate in the Oklahoma Land Rush two decades before the *Dawes Act* opened the door to black settlers. Gurley risked his entire fortune on the move. When the moment came, O.W. and Emma raced amidst the maniacal "stampede"[26] and found their spot of choice after a hysterical 50-mile ride. Their property claim was to become the community of Perry, Oklahoma, one of the territory's new black towns.

**Gurley**

A driven person of seemingly limitless energy, Gurley ran for County Treasurer and served as the principal of the local school. In the same period, he opened a general store. However, some part of him remained unsatisfied as he heard rumors of "giant oil fields"[27] creating great wealth in Tulsa, 80 miles away. Moving to the larger city that year, where black land ownership was still a curiosity, he pursued his profession as both educator and real estate entrepreneur. Without hesitation, he purchased his first large tracts intended for both businesses and residences.

Before the advent of statehood, Gurley's agenda ran headlong into the new state government's first piece of legislation, Senate Bill #1. This act prevented black residents from residing, traveling, and marrying"[28] outside of their race. Also known as the "coach law,"[29] the penalty for

---

[26] Antoine Gara, The Bezos of Black Wall Street, Forbes – www.forbes.com/peter/antoinegara/2020/06/18the-bezos-of-black-wall-street-tulsa-race-riots-1921/#5b37f7c7f321

[27] Antoine Gara

a violation ranged from $100-$1000. Two Republicans voted against the Act, supporting the law but in an emergency bill. They objected to the permission of black doctors and nurses to enter white railroad cars, even in an emergency.

The lines of Gurley's newly purchased property ran from Pine Street in the north to the Frisco Railroad tracks to the south, Lansing Avenue in the east to Cincinnati Avenue at the western end. His first business was a rooming house on a dusty trail near the Frisco tracks. Gurley himself named the road Greenwood Ave. in honor of the city in Mississippi. The boarding house was to become popular for blacks escaping the oppression of Mississippi, arriving by train on a regular basis, and the district's moniker was perhaps intended to present a new version of the Southern locale. The black community created by his efforts was the best of the all-black communities in the country since the years of the Civil War. Although Oklahoma housed nearly all of them, the difference between Greenwood and its contemporary communities was that persecution of black residents was a distant reality, virtually non-existent.

Gurley went on to build three two-story buildings and five residences, purchasing another 80 acres of farmland in Rogers County. In addition, he founded what is now known as the Vernon African Methodist Episcopal Church. The racial climate rendered black residents unable to shop anywhere but Greenwood, a reality that only served to expand the district more quickly. By 1913, many more businesses had become established with the financial help of the city's most prominent bankers. These included the law offices of Buck Colbert Franklin and of physician A.C. Jackson. Two schools appeared, Dunbar and Booker T. Washington High School. The educational system was excellent by any comparison with the rest of the state. Freshmen studied algebra, Latin, and ancient history along with English, science, and music. Sophomores studied economics and geometry. For juniors, the curriculum emphasized trade-oriented subjects. Seniors studied physics and trigonometry, vocal music, art, and bookkeeping. So important was the educational component of the district that teachers were among the most highly paid workers. Many had Steinway pianos in their apartments, considered by much of the world as the king of pianos at the equivalent price of a luxury car or small home.

The Mount Zion Baptist Church took its place next to the Vernon AME to accommodate the enormous Southern Baptist denomination. At its full state of development, the Greenwood district came to house 22 churches. Ricketts' Restaurant became a landmark for dining out and the first Dreamland Theater was constructed by the Williams family within easy reach of the Mann's Grocery Stores. The prodigious Stradford Hotel, built by J.B. Stradford, was accompanied by haberdasheries, drug stores, cafés, barber shops and beauty salons, with a host of essential and luxury shops. In time, insurance companies were added to the Directory, and a skating rink was built.

---

[28] Black Wall Street.org

[29] Oklahoma Historical Society, Senate Bill One – okhistory.com/publications/enc/entry/php?entry=SE017

J.B. (John Baptist) Stradford arrived in Tulsa only two years after Gurley, with his wife Augusta. The two men entered into a partnership dedicated to the district's development despite some differences of approach. They shared a mutual "distrust of white people,"[30] and accordingly, began the Greenwood practice of employing only their initials. For whites to address black men by their first name was considered a form of derision.

**Stradford**

Stradford was the son of a former slave from Versailles, Kentucky, his father having been named Caesar by his owner. Befriended by the owner's daughter, Caesar eventually learned to read the Emancipation Proclamation that set him free. However, he first petitioned his master individually. On a journey from Kentucky to Ontario, he was set free and given the name of Stratford which he altered to Stradford. Working and saving, Caesar eventually obtained the liberty of his entire family, including his son J.B. The first-born son grew up to become a University of Indiana graduate, training as an attorney specializing in "social justice and racial solidarity to real estate."[31] In additional legal studies, Augusta and J.B. were the only African Americans to enter and finish the law curriculum at Oberlin College.

Despite the relative safety of Greenwood during its development, Stradford was well aware that "in Oklahoma, it [was] not considered a crime for a mob to kill a negro."[32] He was an unconstrained voice against Jim Crow in Oklahoma, and typified the aggressive Greenwood response to racial insult. The occasional white visitor was astonished at the black lack of tolerance for remarks and epithets that would have elicited bowing and scraping in other

[30] Shomari Wills, Origins of Black Wall Street, Jan. 10, 2020, Investopedia – www.investopedia.com/insights/origins-black-wall-street/

[31] Black Wall Street, Centennial: Tulsa Pilgrimage, 2021, The Stradfords of Black Wall Street, Tulsa – www.blackwallstrett.org/jbstradford

[32] Thomas F. Armstrong

communities, and by other men. Such an example was driven home when a white deliveryman hurled an offensive quip at Stradford on the street. Before he realized what had happened, Stradford had thrown him to the ground and proceeded to "straddle him and punch his face until it was bloody."[33] Not surprisingly, Stradford was charged with assault, but considering that the deliveryman had insulted him on hallowed ground for the African American, an acquittal was quickly handed down.

Stradford believed that a general success was to be achieved in a black community through the pooling of resources, collaborations in which fellow entrepreneurs were mutually supportive. As had Gurley, Stradford purchased large tracts of acreage in the northeast section of Tulsa, subdivided them and sold them exclusively to African Americans. A number of other speculators followed suit. In the spirit of mutual support, businesses were serviced by colleagues from the community and their establishments instead of relying on resources from white Tulsa. One company, the Acme Brick Works, reaped the benefits of serving as the primary brick construction service in the district, and its work can be seen in nearly every structure of the 35-block commercial zone. While the African American money was being pooled, many in the district still worked for white employers, but did not allow any of their income to remain on the white side of the tracks. This form of "double-saving" grew the coffers silently and rapidly.

In a short time, Stradford's enterprises in the Greenwood District included two dozen rental properties worth a modern sum of two million. His mammoth hotel at 301 N. Greenwood, the largest black-owned hotel in America, stood as the "crown jewel,"[34] with 54 modern living rooms, a gambling hall, dining room, saloon, and pool hall. The Stradford Hotel was noted for its performances of jazz, along with the local Commodore Club. Greenwood was the town in which a young Count Basie first "encountered big-band jazz."[35] For a time, these celebrations could be held without repercussions. However, jazz was an almost embryonic art form in that era, and unsettling to the white population. Traditional Christians across the tracks labeled halls where such music was played as dens of iniquity, adding religious indignation to their resentment of a black community's superior wealth. Stradford was a marked man for his litigation against the railroad as well, as he fought for accommodations due the black traveler. He further "stirred the pot"[36] by railing against Jim Crow and in particular, segregation. His outrage against lynching of "peace loving"[37] neighbors by mobs was unconstrained.

[33] Shomari Wills

[34] Black Wall Street

[35] Black Past, Deep Greenwood (Tulsa) Oklahoma (1906-) – www.blackpast.org/African American-history/deep-greenwood-tulsa-1906/

[36] Black Wall Street

[37] Black Wall Street

**The Stradford Hotel**

Tulsa historian Scott Ellsworth, in *Death in the Promised Land*, recalls a time in which young Bill Williams asked his father why the family had moved from Mississippi to Tulsa. John's response was simply, "I came out to the Promised Land."[38] John Wesley and Loula Tom Williams were wise to make the move, although as two of the earliest residents, little infrastructure was present by the time of their arrival at the turn of the century. The U.S. Census lists the couple as having been married five years. No black doctors had yet become established in Greenwood, and the hospital was not yet built. At the birth of their son William, the couple traveled to Hot Springs, Arkansas for the delivery.

John Williams had an extraordinary talent for machines of every sort, and for a time operated the chilling equipment for the Thompson Ice Cream Company. He was paid so well that he was eventually able to purchase the first automobile in Greenwood. Photos exist of the couple, with Bill in the back seat, sitting in their Chalmers Thirty Pony Tonneau. The thirty horsepower vehicle cost $1,600, the equivalent of $53,000 in modern currency, featuring a three-speed manual transmission and a top speed of 50 mph. Williams made all the repairs of the strange new contraption himself, and was so proficient at maintaining it that others started to bring their cars from Greenwood and the white section of town. Within a few years, John compiled a clientele list that enabled him to let go of his job at the ice cream company and open a garage. At 420 E. Archer Street, in the middle of the financial action, Loula opened a confectionary where candied ice cream was offered and quit her teaching job. Adding an extensive soda fountain, the project was solely "Loula's baby,"[39] and a wildly popular one. The establishment became the central meeting place for the young, and it is said that in the intimate décor, "there were more proposals for marriage…than at any other place in the city."[40] As John's garage brought in handsome

[38] Carlos Moreno, The Victory of Greenwood: John and Loula Williams – www.thevictoryofgreenwood.com/2020/03/15/the-victory-of-greenwood-john-and-loula-greenwood/

[39] Jennifer Latham.com, The Dreamland – www.jenniferlatham.com/?p=248

[40] Jennifer Latham.com

profits, he stayed busy constructing a three-story building to house apartments and office space to go along with the confectionary.

**John and Loula Williams**

Loula's successful venture left her with a taste for more, and the couple's next goal was to provide Greenwood with a theater. In short order, their Empress Theatre opened in 1913 at 17 West 3rd Street. The Empress was no modest example, seating nearly 800 and featuring performances of stage musicals and vaudeville acts. She added a second theater that would become an iconic landmark even in Tulsa's present day, the Dreamland Theatre. In a case of ideal timing, the second theater paralleled the growth of the film industry. In addition to the infancy of Hollywood, black film companies abounded in the eastern half of the country, from Chicago to Florida. Closest to Tulsa was the Lincoln Motion Picture Company of Omaha. At the Dreamland, new movie-goers saw the much-anticipated film entitled *The Green-Eyed Monster*, with an all-black cast. The Williams fortune continued to grow with investments in other communities and John and Loula were to remain among the leading power couples of the community. The Dreamland was eventually burned to the ground in the coming race riots, but despite the insurance company's refusal to resurrect the theater, she had two others in Muskogee and Okmulgee.

Among the most important components of a community intending to chart its own course was a newspaper to serve the black community, defend their agenda, and resist injustice. Throughout the Midwest, South, and East, newspapers were in nearly all cases dominated by the Republican Party's world view as the parties gradually switched the liberal-conservative positions. In Greenwood, *The Tulsa Star* emerged as the only "staunchly Democratic African American paper"[41] in the nation. In addition to its attention to local urges and exterior warnings, the *Star* was at all times promotive of the district's achievements. First on a weekly basis, then as a daily, the community's creation of hospitals, schools, theaters, and churches was trumpeted throughout the region.

The creator, editor and publisher of *The Tulsa Star* was Andrew Jackson Smitherman, who has been described as "spirited and bold…sometimes known to swim against the tide."[42]   In the beginning, Smitherman was wary of the district's "founding fathers," and in particular O.W. Gurley, whose authority seemed overblown. He was fond of referring to the town giant as "the King of Little Africa."[43] His early career was spent as a traveling agent and advertising manager for the distinctly Republican *Muskogee Cimeter*, published by William Henry Twine. Smitherman published his first paper four year later, *The Muskogee Star*, advocating "self-reliance"[44] for all black enclaves, and championing all black causes. Smitherman railed against racism in all of its manifestations. When Republican news organizations claimed that black leaders preferred Jim Crow transportation laws, the leader of the *Star* shot back that if such were true, these supposed black leaders were "ripe for a full coat of tar and feathers."[45] The community's possession of such an important voice was especially true as white Tulsa began to awaken to the district's wealth. In 1914, a law was passed in the city that prohibited any person from living on a block where three quarters of the residency was of a different race, maintaining racial purity in every district, especially the predominantly white one.

Smitherman was at the least one of Greenwood's most outspoken and occasionally colorful characters. Through the years, many articles were printed about the editor himself, uncommon in the industry. A few included "Smitherman shoots at Flour Thief," "Smitherman and His Family," "Smitherman and Dewey Riot," and "Smitherman v. Rioters*.* " In his fight for social justice, Smitherman took the trouble to meet with the governor on more than one occasion. His was the only paper to cover Governor James B.A. Robertson's "inter-racial conference."[46] In addition to his duties at the newspaper, he was appointed Justice of the Peace as well.

When he lost everything in the 1921 race riot, Smitherman returned to run papers in Massachusetts and Buffalo, New York. An indictment based on white accusations that his paper ignited the riots hung over Smitherman's head for years, and he was under threat of immediate death if he ever returned to Tulsa. The Smitherman descendants, still residing in the Tulsa area, have been active in politics by coming to the forefront to discourage a public rally for President Donald Trump in the city. For all the grit in Smitherman's resistance to injustice, he was recalled

---

[41] Oklahoma Historical Society the Gateway to Oklahoma History, Tulsa Star – www.gateway.oklahomahistory.org/explore/collections/TULSA/

[42] Randy Krehbiel, Tulsa Race Massacre, Tulsa World – www.tulsaworld.com/tulsa-race-massacre-led-by-its-determined-editor-tulsa-star-challenged-racism-and-fought-against/article_ccbf6327-422c-5160-be57-c951c237d382.html

[43] Shomari Wills

[44] Oklahoma Historical Society

[45] Randy Krehbiel

[46] Randy Krehbiel

as a warm family man, a quality that aroused his grandchildren to further his struggle. Those who knew their illustrious ancestor still remember him as a clever man filled with "wonderful ghost stories."[47]

The Greenwood District had every profession that one might find in a full-sized city, including an able group of attorneys accustomed to difficult times in white courtrooms. The most notable of these was Buck Colbert Franklin. Unlike most of his contemporaries, he did not migrate from the South, having been born in the town of Homer, Oklahoma. This placed him in the midst of Pickens County of the Chickasaw Nation, in the Indian Territory. He was named Buck in honor of his grandfather, although some believed that the elder Franklin escaped from his plantation and changed his name. As a young man, Franklin practiced law in Ardmore, Oklahoma, and not surprisingly, he often struggled to hold his ground within the white judicial system. He was once utterly silenced in a Louisiana courtroom solely on the basis of his race. In time, he married Mollie Parker and moved to the Greenwood District shortly before the riot. By that time, the district was "among the most affluent black communities in the nation."[48] He is most noted for representing several of the Tulsa survivors of the riot. Franklin's son, John Hope, was hailed for his reappraisal of the Civil War, and he assisted with the Supreme Court brief that resulted in *Brown v. Board of Education of Topeka.*

[47] Sean Kirst, In Buffalo, a hero journalist in Oklahoma found new life after Tulsa massacre, Buffalo News – www.buffalonews.com/news/local/in-buffalo-a-hero-journalist-found-new-life-after-tulsa-massacre/article_a9d2b6cb-0188-50d7-bref-04245-304a9df.html

# Franklin

Among the most essential components for such an enclave was public transportation, and Greenwood was blessed with the presence of Simon Berry, who devised a "nickel-a-ride" plan in a topless Model T. Ford. Further, he established a mass transit system of multiple buses so highly functional that the city of Tulsa eventually purchased it from him. The routes took riders all the way into Tulsa. He owned the Royal Hotel as well, and he regularly shuttled wealthy oil barons in his charter airline service. At the peak of his success, Berry is said to have earned over $500 per day. Tulsans will note that he created what is now known as Lincoln Park and built the first swimming pool in the city, along with other recreational facilities.

For medical service, the Lincoln Hospital came to serve the district admirably, in part due to the presence of Andrew C. Jackson, local physician and surgeon. The Mayo brothers, of Mayo Clinic fame, once asserted that Jackson was "the most able negro surgeon in America."[49] With such a reputation, he instilled a great sense of trust in all that he met, and he treated both races, an astonishing fact in the era.

To note the success of the district by the hands of so many "heavy hitters" brought together is not to say that the town was blithely unconcerned for its safety with white neighbors so near across the tracks. Other "Black Wall Streets" had come to grief, and the general community in Greenwood was well-aware of recent events elsewhere. On occasion, the district itself experienced individual cases of violence. In one instance, a white taxi driver was abducted and shot. The suspect was arrested and lynched, reminding the enclave of the "violent context"[50] in which they lived. Also fresh in the memory were past incidents in which successful black businessmen came to a bad end by doing too well. Only a few years before the establishment of Greenwood, two Memphis grocers were lynched out of envy at their success. According to *The Guardian*, the two men "died on the altar of capitalism."[51] The message was clear: "black entrepreneurism has limits."[52]

## Unrest

As the First World War began to reach its conclusion, East St. Louis, Illinois was the scene of one of the nation's worst race riots, a progression that followed a typical pattern. On February 4, 1917, 470 black workers arrived at the Aluminum Ore Company to replace striking white workers. After formal complaints of black worker migrations were filed, news broke of an attempted robbery of a white man perpetrated by a black man. White mobs formed and

---

[49] Hannibal B. Johnson, Author, Attorney, Consultant, The Ghosts of Greenwood Past, A Walk Down Black Wall Street, May 11, 2019 – www.hannibaljohnson.com/the-ghosts-of-greenwood-past-a-walk-down-black-wall-street

[50] Thomas F. Armstrong

[51] The Guardian, In 1921, A White Mob Burned Black Wall Street Down. We Still Feel That Legacy Today – www.guardian.com/comments is free/2020/jun/19/tulsa-1921-massacre-trump-violence-legacy/

[52] The Guardian

"rampaged through downtown,"[53] beating every black person who could be found. Trolleys and streetcars were stopped, and black riders were pulled out and severely beaten. As was typical in such events, Illinois' leaders called out the National Guard, and as it turned out, this was only the prelude to heightened violence erupting a few days later. Black homes were burned to the ground, and men, women, and children were beaten and shot to death.

On July 27, 1919, an African American teenager drowned in Lake Michigan after violating the unofficial segregation policy of Chicago's beaches. He was stoned by a group of white youths, bringing on what has been termed "The Red Summer." The police were called, but they refused to make an arrest, although the primary suspect was pointed out. That sparked a week of rioting between black and white Chicagoans in a South Side neighborhood near the stockyards, resulting in 15 whites and 23 blacks killed, as well as 500 people injured. An additional 1,000 black families lost their homes after they were torched by rioters. The violence was the culmination of rising tension as larger black migrations moved from the South to northern cities in search of work. Simultaneously, thousands of veterans returned home from Europe, only to find their factory jobs filled with Southern blacks and immigrants. The return of black veterans carried an added slight, as African American servicemen were excluded from the GI Bill.

In a period of financial instability, deep cultural prejudices ran rampant throughout the country. To exacerbate the situation, the KKK reinitiated a reign of terror in Southern cities and managed to work their way up to Chicago where the African American population in the city had grown to 100,000. As was usually the case, the state militia was called in, but President Woodrow Wilson blamed the black newcomers as "lawless instigators."[54]

The Klan inevitably arrived in Tulsa as well, where a success story such as Greenwood was a magnet for the organization's racist violence, but before the 1921 riot, the rigidity of segregation helped the renowned entrepreneurial center of Greenwood avoid the social catastrophes exploding in other cities. The financial sector bloomed quickly with few peripheral crises. The influx of new black settlers that followed required an expansion of facilities including service businesses, schools, and entertainment centers. By 1920, black settlers had established 50 black communities scattered throughout the state of Oklahoma.

Once established, Tulsa became a lively locale for Klan activity. It is estimated that in December 1921, the Tulsa Klan had 3,200 members out of a population of around 72,000 in 1920. Clark described the growth of the Klan in Tulsa: "Kleagles capitalized upon the emotions in the wake of the race riot to propagandize the white community of Tulsa. The result was astounding. Soon the Tulsa Klan Number Two boasted of 2,000 members. The Klavern, the smallest local unit of the organizational structure wherein the ritual ceremonies were held, grew so rapidly that in six months the Klan paid an estimated $60,000 for the Centenary Methodist

[53] Black Past, East St. Louis Race Riot, 1917 – www.blackpast.org/African American-history/east-st-louis race-riot-1917/

[54] History.com, The Red Summer of 1919 – www.history.com/black-history/chicago-race-riot0of-1919

Church building in Tulsa and built one of the largest meeting halls in the Southwest on the spot. Civil leaders formed formed the Tulsa Benevolent Association in January, 1922. It served as the holding company for the Tulsa Klan under the leadership of the Exalted Cyclops, who was William Shelley Rogers, and included many of the prominent business, professional, and local government leaders of the region. Tulsa gossips passed along the common rumor that all district judges, the court clerk, the county sheriff, and all jury commissioners were members of the Klan."

Given that the growth of the Ku Klux Klan among the white citizens of Tulsa came mostly after the riot, the group itself can't be directly blamed. Instead, the riot was an outgrowth of racial and social tensions in the city that mirrored those in other areas in the aftermath of World War I. The return of black soldiers to urban areas in 1918 prompted worries among whites, who feared that lawless black mobs would threaten the safety and stability of their cities. Riots broke out in Northern cities, with whites rampaging through black commercial and residential areas, burning black-owned properties and killing and injuring men, women and children.

While there was not an outbreak of racial violence in Tulsa that summer, the pattern of the later riot in that city mirrored that of Chicago, with white mobs rampaging through black areas of the city in response to rumored violence and other activities that (theoretically) defied white supremacy. By 1921, tensions arising from a variety of factors threatened to fan racial animosities. The report commented, "Despite the fact that segregation appeared to be gaining ground statewide, in the months leading up to the riot, more than a few white Tulsans instead feared, at least in Tulsa itself, that the opposite was true. Many were especially incensed when black Tulsans disregarded, or challenged, Jim Crow practices. Others were both enraged at, and jealous of, the material success of some of Greenwood's leading citizens--feelings that were no doubt increased by the sharp drop in the price of crude oil, and the subsequent layoffs in the oil fields, that preceded the riot. Indeed, an unidentified writer for one white Tulsa publication, the Exchange Bureau Bulletin, later listed 'n*****s with money' as one of the so-called causes of the catastrophe. During the weeks and months leading up to the riot, there were more than a few white Tulsans who not only feared that the color line was in danger of being slowly erased, but believed that this was already happening."

Joined with this concern among whites that their dominance was in danger was a growing concern about crime and vice in Tulsa. A federal agent who spent a week undercover in Tulsa in April 1921, a month before the outbreak of the riot, reported, "Gambling, bootlegging and prostitution are very much in evidence. At the leading hotels and rooming houses the bell hops and porters are pimping for women and also selling booze. Regarding violations of the law, these prostitutes and pimps solicit without any fear of the police, as they will invariably remind you that you are safe in these houses...Vice conditions in this city are extremely bad."

Growing concern about crime, particularly violations of prohibition laws, led to an anti-crime movement in the city spurred by the city's newspapers, which editorialized against vice and crime in increasingly racial tones. The *Tulsa Tribune* led the way, but the commission's report claimed, "Despite later claims to the contrary, for much of early 1921, race had not been much of a factor in the *Tribune's* vigorous anti-crime and anti-corruption campaign."

The paper had not highlighted crimes in Greenwood to a greater degree than other areas of the city, nor did they focus on black criminals disproportionately, but the paper stoked racial tensions shortly before the riot occurred that summer: "But beginning on May 21, 1921, only ten days before the riot, all that was to change. In a lengthy, front-page article...not only did racial issues suddenly come to the foreground, but more importantly, they did so in a manner that featured the highly explosive subject of relations between black men and white women...Accompanied by a private detective [Reverend Harold G. Cooke, the white pastor of Centenary Methodist Church] had led a small group of white men on an undercover tour of the city's illicit nightlife--and had been, it was reported, horrified at what he had discovered...Not only was liquor available at every place that they visited, but at hotels and rooming houses across the city. It was said, African American porters rather routinely offered to provide the men with the services of white prostitutes. Just beyond the city limits, the *Tribune* reported, the group visited a roadhouse where the color lines seemed to have disappeared entirely. 'We found whites and Negroes singing and dancing together,' one member of Reverend Cook's party testified, 'Young, white girls were dancing while Negroes played.'"

All of this coverage gave white Tulsans a new target for their concerns: black men who in their view had too much contact with white women. The commission report noted: "By the end of May 1921, an unstable and potentially volatile local atmosphere. For more than a few white Tulsans, local conditions regarding crime and punishment were fast becoming intolerable. Frustrated over the amount of lawbreaking in their city, and by the apparent inability of the police to do anything about it, they had helped turn the city into a ticking time bomb, where anger and frustration sat just beneath the surface, waiting to explode."

At the same time, Greenwood residents had a growing determination themselves: "[T]here were black Tulsans who were more determined than ever than in their city, no African-American would fall victim to mob violence. World War I veterans and newspaper editors, common laborers and businessmen, they were just as prepared as they had been two years earlier to make certain that no black person was ever lynched in Tulsa, Oklahoma."

The pieces were thus in place for an explosion.

### The Mob Gathers

Given their importance at the center of events leading to the Tulsa riot, there is very little known about either Dick Rowland or Sara Page.

Rowland, the young black man spotted running from the Drexel Building, is presumed to have been 19 at the time. His place of birth is unknown, but it is known his name at birth was Jimmie Jones, and by 1908 he and his two sisters had been orphaned. Jimmie was taken in by Damie Ford, and around 1909 Ford moved herself and Jimmie to Tulsa and moved in with Ford's family, the Rowlands. Jimmie took Rowland as his last name and adopted Dick as his first name. He attended Booker T. Washington High School, but he dropped out before graduating. Rowland took a job shining shoes at a white-owned and white-patronized shine parlor on Main Street. It was there that he was working on May 30, 1921.

Even less is known about Sarah Page. She was 17-years-old and worked as an elevator operator at the Drexel Building, a job typically reserved for women at the time. It is believed she came to Tulsa from Missouri and lived in a rented room located on North Boston Avenue. There have been reports that she was attending a local business school at the time.

# The Drexel Building

The elevator of the Drexel Building that Page operated was the only one in the building, and Rowland would have had a perfectly legitimate reason for wanting to use the elevator. The segregation of facilities in Tulsa was so strict that the shine parlor had no toilet facilities for its black employees. Instead, the owner of the parlor had arranged for his employees to use the closest "Colored" restroom, which happened to be located on the fifth floor of the Drexel Building. In order to get there, Rowland would have had to use the elevator.

Since the arrangement made by his employer had been in place for a long time, it has led to speculation that Rowland and Page knew each other before that day. The commission report explained, "It seems reasonable that they would have least been able to recognize each other on sight, as Rowland would have regularly ridden in Page's elevator on his way to and from the restroom. Others, however, have speculated that the pair might have been lovers – a dangerous and potentially deadly taboo, but not an impossibility...Whether they knew each other or not, it is clear that both Dick Rowland and Sarah Page were downtown on Monday, May 30, 1921 – although this, too, is cloaked in some mystery. On Memorial Day, most – but not all – stores and businesses in Tulsa were closed. Yet, both Rowland and Page were apparently working that day."

The only thing that is not subject to speculation is that at some point on Memorial Day, Rowland entered the elevator Page was operating in the Drexel Building. It is what happened next that has been the object of speculation since that day. The most commonly believed explanation was that Rowland tripped as he got on the elevator and grabbed Page by the arm to break his fall. Page, likely startled, screamed in response. Those who knew Rowland insisted that this was the most likely explanation, and that the young man would never have been capable of rape.

The clerk working at Renberg's, however, drew the opposite conclusion. Hearing a woman's screams and seeing a young black man appear to run from the building, the clerk rushed to the elevator and found Page. Perceiving her to be distraught, the clerk decided that she was the victim of an attempted sexual assault and called the police.

The official police record is vague about what happened next. The clerk apparently stuck to his story, but there is no record of what Page told the police when they interviewed her. Based on the actions the police took next, it does not appear that whatever Page told them was interpreted as an attempted sexual assault by a black male on a white female. The police did not issue an all-points bulletin for Rowland, but instead kept the investigation low-key. Rowland, for his part, went to his adopted mother's home and hid out, no doubt fearful of being set upon by a white lynch mob.

Whatever investigation the police did, the next morning, May 31, Tulsa police arrested

Rowland. One of the arresting officers, Patrolman Henry C. Pack, was among the few black members of the 75 on the city police force. Police booked Rowland at police headquarters, and he was initially held at the city jail. He was moved later that day to the county jail, located on the top floor of the Tulsa County Courthouse, after police received an anonymous threat on Rowland's life. Damie Ford lost no time hiring a prominent white attorney to defend her adopted son. Rowland was known to quite a few of the lawyers in Tulsa who frequented the parlor where he worked, and at least one of the attorneys in town was overheard saying, "I don't believe a damn word of it. Why I know the boy and have known him a good long while. That's not in him."

**The courthouse**

Eventually, Rowland's arrest caught the attention of the afternoon paper of record in Tulsa, the *Tulsa Tribune*. The *Tribune* published an article about the arrest on its front page with the headline, "Nab Negro for Attacking Girl in an Elevator." Part of the article told readers, "A Negro delivery boy who gave his name to the public as 'Diamond Dick' but who has been identified as Dick Rowland, was arrested on South Greenwood Avenue this morning by Officers Carmichael and Pack, charged with attempting to assault the 17-year-old white elevator girl in the Drexel Building early yesterday. He will be tried in municipal court this afternoon on a state charge. The girl said she noticed the Negro a few minutes before the attempted assault looking up and down the hallway on the third floor of the Drexel Building as if to see if there was anyone in in sight but thought nothing of it at the time. A few minutes later he entered the elevator she claimed, and attacked her, scratching her hands and face and tearing her clothes. Her screams brought a clerk from Renberg's store to her assistance and the Negro fled. He was captured and identified this morning both by the girl and the clerk, police say. Tenants of the Drexel Building said the girl is an orphan who works as an elevator operator to pay her way through business college."

# Nab Negro for Attacking Girl In an Elevator

A negro delivery boy who gave his name to the police as "Diamond Dick" but who has been identified as Dick Rowland, was arrested on South Greenwood avenue this morning by Officers Carmichael and Pack, charged with attempting to assault the 17-year-old white elevator girl in the Drexel building early yesterday.

He will be tried in municipal court this afternoon on a state charge.

The girl said she noticed the negro a few minutes before the attempted assault looking up and down the hallway on the third floor of the Drexel building as if to see if there was anyone in sight but thought nothing of it at the time.

A few minutes later he entered the elevator she claimed, and attacked her, scratching her hands and face and tearing her clothes. Her screams brought a clerk from Renberg's store to her assistance and the negro fled. He was captured and identified this morning both by the girl and clerk, police say.

Rowland denied that he tried to harm the girl, but admitted he put his hand on her arm in the elevator when she was alone.

Tenants of the Drexel building said the girl is an orphan who works as an elevator operator to pay her way through business college.

Where the *Tribune* got the description of the incident that they ascribed to Sarah Page is unknown, since there is no known record of such a statement to the police. It is possible this was what they received from the store clerk, or one of the reporters may have simply made it up.

There is a further mystery about what the *Tribune* printed in its pages. There is no complete run of the bound volumes of the newspaper. The microfilm version does contain the issue of

May 31, 1921, but before the issue was microfilmed, the article that appeared on the front page was torn out along with the bulk of the editorial page. A copy was found by Loren Gill for his 1946 Master's thesis on the riot and reprinted in its entirety, and another copy is in the Red Cross papers that are part of the collections of the Tulsa Historical Society. A copy of what was printed on the editorial page has never been located, however.

Witnesses to the events surrounding the riot remembered the *Tribune* mentioning the possibility of a lynching. One person recalled, in an interview shortly after the riot, "The *Daily Tribune*, a white newspaper that tries to gain its popularity by referring to the Negro settlement as 'Little Africa,' came out on the evening of Tuesday, May 31, with an article claiming that a Negro had experienced some trouble with a white elevator girl at the Drexel Building, it also said that a mob of whites was forming in order to lynch the Negro."

The talk of lynching Rowland was reported shortly after the *Tribune* report. By 4:00, Police and Fire Commissioner J.F. Adkinson telephoned Sheriff Willard McCullough and alerted him to the rumors. Fueling these rumors, a crowd of white residents began to gather around the Tulsa County Courthouse at Sixth and Boulder, and by sunset the crowd had swelled to several hundred. The new sheriff of Tulsa County, Willard M. McCullough, took steps to ensure Rowland's safety. He organized his deputies in a defensive perimeter around the prisoner, disabled the building's elevator, positioned six deputies with rifles and shotguns on the roof, and ordered his remaining men to guard the top of the stairs and shoot anyone on sight. McCullough stood on the courthouse steps and tried to get the mob to go home, but he was reportedly shouted down. Three men entered the courthouse and demanded the sheriff turn Rowland over before they were turned away.

**McCullough**

## The Riot

While the white mob was surrounding the courthouse and Sheriff McCullough was doing his best to protect Rowland's life, news of what was going on spread to Greenwood. There was some dispute among the community as to the proper response to take. At the Dreamland Theater, a man jumped onto the stage. "We're not going to let this happen," he declared. "We're going to go downtown and stop this lynching. Close this place down." B. C. Franklin later recalled two war veterans exhorting a crowd to go downtown to stop the lynching. The commission report explained, "What went unspoken was the fact an African-American had never been lynched in Tulsa. How to prevent one from taking place now was no easy matter...exactly how to respond was of utmost concern." A.J. Smitherman, editor of the *Tulsa Star*, urged action, saying, "Come on boys, let's go downtown."

On the other hand, O. W. Gurley, the owner of the Gurley Hotel, and Barney Cleaver, a black deputy sheriff, counseled caution. Gurley would later tell the grand jury investigating the riot, "I saw a bunch of negroes the night of the riot starting up town and I told them to go back home; the first knowledge I had of it was from Mr. A. F. Bryant; I went upstairs and when I came back down I saw John Smithisen, and he said we will go to the Star office; I went away and when I came back in ¾ of an hour 50 or 60 men were armed with rifles; I asked them to go home, and told them there was no danger of a lynching, and one fellow said that is a damn lie, Mr. McCullough just called for us."

What happened next is somewhat murky. Grand jury testimony would later claim that a group of 50 or 60 black veterans armed with rifles and shotguns arrived at the jail to support Sheriff McCullough (the commission report decades later put the number at 25). In any event, regardless of the exact number, the men marched from their cars to the courthouse steps. Attorney General James Luther would later tell the grand jury, "I saw a car full of negroes driving through the streets with guns; I saw Bill McCullough and told him those negroes would cause trouble; McCullough tried to talk to them, and they got out and stood in single file. W. G. Daggs was killed near Boulder and Sixth street. I was under the impression that a man with authority could have stopped and disarmed them. I saw Chief of Police on south side of court house on top step, talking; I did not see any officer except the Chief; I walked in the court house and met McCullough in about 15 feet of his door; I told him these negroes were going to make trouble, and he said he had told them to go home; he went out and told the whites to go home, and one said 'they said you told them to come up here.' McCullough said 'I did not' and a negro said you did tell us to come."

McCullough was able to persuade the men that Rowland was safe, and that there was no danger of him being turned over to be lynched. Satisfied, the men returned to Greenwood, but the sight of armed black men incited the white mob, which now numbered an estimated 1,000 people. Many of the whites went home to retrieve their own guns, and some headed to the National Guard Armory.

Major James A. Bell, who had already alerted his guardsmen to report to the armory in case they were needed, was informed that a mob of white men was attempting to break into the armory. He later reported, "About 9 o'clock P M. on May 31st. Two members of the guard...came to my door and reported that a crowd of white mem were gathering near the Court House, and that threats of lynching a negro were being made, and that it was reported the negroes in 'Little Africa' were arming to prevent it. As I had heard rumors of this kind on other occasions that did not amount to anything serious I did not feel greatly worried. However, I instructed these men to return to town and get all the information they could; see what the crowd was doing; whether they were armed or not and report back to me at the Armory. I then went to the Armory and called up the Sheriff and asked if there was any indications of trouble down there. The sheriff reported that there were some threats but did not believe it would amount to anything, that in any event he could protect his prisoner. I then called the Chief of Police and asked him the same questions. The chief reported that things were a little threatening, that it was reported that negroes were driving around town in a threatening mood. I then notified the commanding officers of the three Tulsa units, who were in the Armory getting ready for camp, to hold all men in the Armory, have them get into their uniforms, get all arms and ammunition ready so that if it became necessary and the Governor called us we would be ready. I, also, notified them to quickly, but quietly, notify all members of the guard to report at the Armory without giving an alarm. I then returned to my home, just across the alley from the Armory, for my uniform. However, before I could get into it a runner came to my door very much excited and reported that a mob was trying to break into the Armory. Grabbing my pistol in one hand and my belt in the other I jumped out of the back door and running down the west side of the Armory building I saw several men apparently pulling at the window grating. Commanding these men to get off the lot and seeing this command obeyed I went to the front of the building near the southwest corner where I saw a mob of white men about three or four hundred strong. I asked them what they wanted. One of them replied 'Rifles and ammunition'. I explained to them that they could not get anything there. Some one shouted 'we don't know about that, we guess we can'. I told them we only had sufficient arms and ammunition for our men and that not one piece could go out of there without orders from the Governor, and in the name of the law demanded that they disperse at once. They continued to press forward in a threatening manner when with drawn pistol I again demanded that they disperse and explained that the men in the Armory were armed with rifles loaded with ball ammunition and that they would shoot promptly to prevent any unauthorized person entering there. By maintaining a firm stand...the mob was dispersed."

Back at the courthouse, the crowd had swelled to more than 2,000 people by 9:30 pm. Reverend Charles W. Kerr of the First Presbyterian Church, among other local leaders, tried to get the mob to disperse. The Police Chief, John A. Gustafson, later claimed that he tried to talk the lynch mob into dispersing, but he was not on the scene by 10:00.

As the evening wore on, blacks in Greenwood became increasingly concerned. Small groups would venture by car to the courthouse to keep tabs on what was going on, and many of the whites at the courthouse interpreted these actions as the beginning of a "negro uprising." At 10:00 p.m., a larger group of armed men, perhaps 75 or more, drove from Greenwood to the courthouse to once again offer their services.

It was at this point that the situation escalated. The commission report described the scene: "As the black men were leaving the courthouse for the second time, a white man approached a tall African-American World War I veteran who was carrying an army-issued revolver. 'N*****,' the white man said, 'What are you doing with that pistol?' 'I'm going to use it if I need to,' replied the black veteran. 'No, you give it to me.' 'Like hell I will.' The white man tried to take the gun away from the veteran, and a shot rang out. America's worst race riot had begun. While the first shot fired at the courthouse may have been unintentional, those that followed were not. Almost immediately, members of the white mob--and possibly some law enforcement officers-- opened fire on the African-American men, who returned volleys of their own. The initial gunplay lasted only a few seconds, but when it was over, an unknown number of people--perhaps as many as a dozen--both black and white, lay dead or wounded."

The black men retreated toward Greenwood with the white mob in close pursuit, while another skirmish broke out at Second and Cincinnati. Although they were outnumbered and suffering some casualties during the retreat, the black men were able to make it to safety in Greenwood.

The white mob around the courthouse now transformed itself from a lynch mob focused on one black prisoner to one looking to take out their frustrations on any black target they could. They began to move along the sidewalks downtown, and one witness would later say, "A great many of these persons lining the sidewalks were holding a rifle or shotgun in one hand, and grasping the neck of a liquor bottle with the other. Some had pistols stuck into their belts." Many were sworn in by police officers as "Special Deputies." Groups of whites began breaking into downtown sporting goods stores and pawnshops to get guns and ammunition.

Armed whites then began gunning down any black person they found downtown. William R. Holway, a white engineer, was watching a movie at the Rialto Theater when someone ran into the theater yelling, "N***** fight! N***** fight!" He recalled, "Everybody left that theater on high, you know. We went out the door and looked across the street, and there was Younkman's drug store with those big pillars. There were two big pillars. There were two big pillars at the entrance, and we got over behind them. Just got there when a Negro ran south of the alley across the street, the minute his head showed outside, somebody shot him. We stood there for about half-an-hour watching which I shall never forget. He wasn't quite dead, but he was about to die. He was the first man I saw shot in that riot."

A white teenager, William Phillips, later described a similar event in the Royal Theater: "The mob action was set off when several [white] men chased a Negro man down the alley in back of the theater and out onto Fourth Street where he saw the stage door and dashed inside. Seeing the open door the Negro rushed in and hurried forward in the darkness hunting a place to hide. Suddenly he was on the stage in front of the picture screen and blinded by the bright flickering light coming down from the operator's booth in the balcony. After shielding his eyes for a moment he regained his vision enough to locate the steps leading from the stage down past the orchestra pit to the aisle just as the pursuing men rushed the stage. One of them saw the Negro and yelled, 'There he is, heading for the aisle.' As he finished the sentence, a roaring blast from a shotgun dropped the Negro man by the end of the orchestra pity."

Sporadic fighting took place throughout the night of May 31-June 1. From midnight until 1:30 a.m., blacks and whites exchanged gunfire across the Frisco yards. A few carloads of whites made excursions into Greenwood, firing into businesses and residences. Walter White, visiting Tulsa immediately after the riot, reported, "Many are the stories of horror told to me--not by colored people--but by white residents. One was that of an aged colored couple, saying their evening prayers before retiring in their little home on Greenwood Avenue. A mob broke into the house, shot both of the old people in the backs of their heads, blowing their brains out and spattering them over the bed, pillaged the home, and then set fire to it."

Whites began burning black homes and businesses along Archer Street, and then they forced away firefighters who arrived to battle the flames. One firefighter later recounted, "It would mean a fireman's life to turn a stream of water on one of those negro buildings. They shot at us all morning when we were trying to do something but none of my men were hit. There is not a chance in the world to get through that mob into the negro district." Two dozen black-owned businesses burned by 4:00 a.m.

Word began to filter back to Greenwood and other black neighborhoods that angry whites were preparing to invade the district. One such report got back to Seymour Williams, a teacher at Booker T. Washington High School and veteran, compelling him to grab his service revolver and alert his neighbors. In another part of Greenwood, theater owner John Wesley Williams loaded his 30-30 rifle and repeating shotgun, positioning himself in the window of his family's second floor apartment at the corner of Greenwood and Archer. Other black Tulsans decided to leave, and in the early hours of June 1 a steady stream left the city. There was widespread confusion as to what was going on throughout the city, but the uncertainty added to the tensions.

In white neighborhoods, groups of armed men began making plans for what to do next. Phillips would later write, "Many people were drifting out of the restaurant so we decided to go along and see what happened at the meeting place. Driving south on boulder we realized that many trucks and automobiles were headed for the same location, and near Fifteenth Street people had abandoned their vehicles because the streets and intersections were filled to capacity. We left the car more than a block away and began walking toward the crowded intersection. There were already three or four hundred people there and more arriving when we walked up."

After he and his friends arrived there, Phillips noted that a man stood up on top of a car and told the crowd, "We have decided to go out to Second and Lewis Streets and join the crowd that is meeting there." Phillips and his friends returned to their cars and headed east with a long line of cars toward Second and Lewis. There, men were shouting instructions to the crowds. One said, "Men, we are going in at daylight." Another told the crowd, "If any of you have more ammunition than you need, or if what you have doesn't fit your gun, sing out." "Be ready at daybreak," a man urged the crowd, adding, "Nothing can stop us for there will be thousands of others going in at the same time."

Meanwhile, state officials in Oklahoma City were learning of the situation in Tulsa. The commission report explained, "At 10:14 pm, Adjutant General Charles F. Barrett, the commandant of the Oklahoma National Guard, had received a long distance telephone call from Major Byron Kirkpatrick, a Tulsa guard officer, advising him of the worsening conditions in Tulsa. Kirkpatrick phoned again at 12:35 a.m. At that point he was instructed by Governor J.B.A. Robertson to prepare and send a signed telegram, as required by Oklahoma state law, by the chief of police, the county sheriff, and a local judge, requesting that state troops be sent to Tulsa. Kirkpatrick, however, ran into some problems as he tried to collect the necessary signatures, particularly that of Sheriff McCullough, who was still barricaded with his men and Dick Rowland on the top floor of the courthouse. However, Kirkpatrick persevered, and at 1:46 a.m. the needed telegram arrived at the state capital."

At 2:15, Adjutant General Barrett told Kirkpatrick that the governor had authorized calling out the National Guard, and a train of nearly 100 guardsmen would be leaving Oklahoma City for Tulsa at 5:00 that morning.

By sunrise on June 1, groups of armed whites numbering in the thousands had gathered in three clusters on the northern fringes of the downtown area opposite Greenwood. Some observers at would later estimate the total number between 5,000-10,000. One small group of men placed a machine gun at the top of Middle State's Milling Company's grain elevator, positioning it to fire on Greenwood Avenue.

In Greenwood, blacks were faced with a stark choice: fight or flee. What happened to Julia Duff, a teacher at Booker T. Washington High School, was later described in a letter in the *Chicago Defender*: "Mrs. S. came into her room and told her to dress-there was something wrong for soldiers were all around, and she looked out the window and saw them driving the men out of the houses on Detroit. Saw Mr. Wood running with both hands in the air and their 3-month-old baby in one hand and three brutes behind him with guns. She said her legs gave way from under her and she had to crawl about the room, taking things from her closet, putting them in her trunk, for she thought if anything happened she'd have her trunk packed, and before she got everything in they heard footsteps on their steps and there were six out there and they ordered Mr. Smart to march, hands up, out of the house."

Eyewitnesses recalled that around dawn that morning at 5:08 am, there was a whistle or siren that could be heard. Moments later, the white mobs began to move, the machine gun on the elevator opened fire, and crowds of whites headed straight for the commercial district. One witness recalled, "With wild frenzied shouts, men began pouring from behind the freight depot and the long string of boxcars and evidently from behind the piles of oil well easing which was at the other end and on the north side of the building. From every place of shelter up and down the tracks came screaming, shouting men to join in the rush toward the Negro section. Mingled with the shouting were a few rebel-yells and Indian gobblings as the great wave of humanity rushed forward totally absorbed in thoughts of destruction." As reporter Mary Parish later put it, "Tuesday Night, May 31, was the riot, and Wednesday morning, by daybreak, was the invasion."

Faced with the overwhelming numbers of whites, the black residents of Greenwood who had initially resolved to defend their homes and businesses now rushed to leave the district, escaping just ahead of the rampaging mob. The experience of Mary Parrish and her young daughter Florence was typical: "My friend, Mrs. Jones, called her husband, who was trying to take a little rest. They decided to try to make for a place of safety, so called to me that they were leaving. By this time the enemy was close upon us, so they ran out of the south door, which led out onto Archer Street, and went east toward Lansing. I took my little girl, Florence Mary, by the hand and fled out of the west door on Greenwood. I did not take time to get a hat for myself or Baby, but started out north on Greenwood, running amidst showers of bullets from the machine gun located in the granary and from men who were quickly surrounding our district. Seeing that they were fighting at a disadvantage, our men had taken shelter in the buildings and in other placed out of sight of the enemy. When my daughter, Florence Mary, and I ran into the street, it was vacant for a block or more. Someone called to me to 'Get out of the street with that child or you both will be killed.' I felt that it was suicide to remain in the building, for it would surely be destroyed and death in the street was preferred, for we expected to be shot down at any moment. So we placed our trust in God, our Heavenly Father, who seeth and knoweth all things, and ran out of Greenwood in the hope of reaching a friend's home who lived over the Standpipe Hill in Greenwood Addition."

As the sun rose, airplanes began to appear overhead. Eyewitnesses reported that the planes, manned by armed whites, flew low to the ground and shot at fleeing blacks. The commission reported noted that the eyewitness accounts are fairly consistent: "Numerous other eyewitnesses--both black and white--confirm the presence of an unknown number of airplanes flying over Greenwood during the early daylight hours of June 1. While certain other assertions made over the years such as that the planes dropped streams of liquid fire on top of African-American homes and businesses appear to have been technologically improbably, particularly during the early 1920s, there is little doubt but that some of the occupants of the airplanes fired upon black Tulsans with pistols and rifles. Moreover, there is evidence to suggest that men in at least one airplane dropped some dynamite, upon a group of African-American refugees as they were fleeing the city."

As the invasion of the Greenwood district unfolded, a pattern began to emerge that the report later described: "First, the armed whites broke into the black homes and businesses, forcing the occupants out into the street, where they were led away at gunpoint to one of a growing number of internment centers. Anyone who resisted was shot. Moreover, African-American men in homes where firearms were discovered met the same fate. Next, the whites looted the homes and businesses, pocketing small items, and hauling away larger items either on foot or by car or truck. Finally, the white rioters then set the homes and other buildings on fire, using torches and oil-soaked rags. House by house, block by block, the wall of flame crept northward, engulfing the city's black neighborhoods."

Witnesses reported that uniformed police and National Guard, rather than seeking to protect life and property, actively engaged in the rioting. These men, along with armed white civilians, also engaged in activities that led to the imprisonment of virtually all of Tulsa's black citizens. James West, a teacher at Booker T. Washington High School, described his arrest by whites at his home on Easton Street: "Some men appeared with drawn guns and ordered all of the men out of the house. I went out immediately. They ordered me to raise my hands, after which three or four men searched me. They told me to line up in the street. I requested them to let me get my hat and best shoes, but they refused and abusively ordered me to line up. They refused to let one of the men put on any kind of shoes. After lining up some 30 or 40 of us men, they ran us through the streets to Convention Hall, forcing us to keep our hands in the air all the while.

While we were running, some of the ruffians would shoot at our heels and swore at those who had difficulty keeping up. They actually drove a car into the bunch and knocked down two or three men."

**A picture of the National Guard with some wounded men during the riot**

**A picture of "Little Africa" on fire**

**A panorama of damage taken from Booker T. Washington High School**

**A picture of damage done on one of Greenwood's residential blocks**

The experience of the respected black surgeon Dr. A. C. Jackson is an example of the atrocities Tulsa's whites meted out on their black neighbors. Jackson was shot by whites and eventually succumbed to his injuries. White attorney John A. Oliphant later testified,

Q. About what time in the morning did you say it was Dr. Jackson was shot?

A. Right close to eight o'clock, between seven thirty and eight o'clock.

Q. Dr. Jackson was a Negro?

A. Yes, sir.

Q. And he was coming toward you and these other men at the time he was shot?

A. Yes, sir, coming right between his house, right in his yard between his home and the house below him.

Q. What did these men say at the time he was shot?

A. They didn't say anything but they pulled down on him; I kept begging him not to shoot him, I held him a good bit and I thought he wouldn't shoot but he shot him twice and the other fellow on the other side-and he fell-shot him and broke his leg.

Q. One man shot him twice?

A. Yes, sir, this is my recollection now.

Q. Then another one shot him through the leg?

A. Yes, I didn't look at that fellow.

Q. These same men that shot him carried him to the hospital?

A. No, they didn't.

Q. What did they do?

A. I have never seen them after that, I don't know a thing about what became of them.

Not all of Tulsa's whites participated in the massacre in the Greenwood area. There are many reports of whites acting heroically to save blacks fleeing the violence. The home of Merrill and Ruth Phelps became a refuge for blacks fleeing Tulsa, as the couple hid and fed refugees in the basement of their home for days. Some whites in Tulsa put their own lives at risk to hide blacks from the rioters, including confronting the armed mobs. Mary Jo Erhard, a white stenographer who lived at the Y.W. C. A., hid the organization's black porter in the building's walk-in refrigerator. She later recalled, "Hardly had I hidden him behind the beef carcasses and returned to the hall door when a loud pounding at the service entrance drew me there. A large man was trying to open the door, fortunately securely locked, and there on the stoop stood three very rough-looking middle aged white men, each pointing a revolver in my general direction! 'What do you want?' I asked sharply. Strangely, those guns frightened me not at all. I was so angry I could have torn those ruffians apart-three armed white men chasing one lone, helpless Negro. I cannot recall in all my life feeling hatred toward any person, until then. Apparently my feelings did not show, for one answered, 'Where did he go?' 'Where did WHO go?' I responded. 'That nigger,' one demanded, 'did you let him in here?' 'Mister,' I said, 'I'm not letting ANYBODY in here!,' which was perfectly true. I had already let in all I intended. It was at least ten minutes before I felt secure enough to release Jack...H was nearly frozen, dressed thinly as he was for the hot summer night, but he was ALIVE!"

The smoke rising from the burning Greenwood area could be seen for miles, and it was already thick in the air when the State National Guard finally arrived in Tulsa from Oklahoma City, the train pulling into Tulsa's Frisco and Santa Fe depot at around 9:15. Their arrival did not put an immediate end to the riot, however, because for reasons that are still unclear, the State Troops did not proceed to the Greenwood area. The commission report found, "The reasons for this seeming hold-up appear to be largely due to the fact that certain steps needed to be fulfilled--either through protocol or by law--in order for martial law to be declared in Tulsa. Accordingly, after detraining at the Frisco and Santa Fe station, Adjutant General Barrett led a detachment of soldiers to the courthouse, where an unsuccessful attempt was made to contact Sheriff McCullough. Barrett then went to city hall, where, after conferring with city officials, he contacted Governor Robertson in Oklahoma City and asked to be granted the authority to proclaim martial law in Tulsa County. Other detachments of State Troops, meanwhile, appear to have begun taking charge of black Tulsans who were being held by armed white civilians. However, another account of the riot, published a decade later, alleges that upon their arrival in Tulsa, the State Troops wasted valuable minutes by taking time to prepare and eat breakfast."

Martial law was finally declared in Tulsa at 11:29 a.m., but by this time, the riot had mostly run its course. There were scattered bands of white rioters continuing to loot and burn, but most of the mob had already gone home, while most of the city's black population continued to be held under armed guard at the Convention Hall, the baseball park, and the fairgrounds. As men, women, and children who had fled to the countryside began to come back into town, they were taken into custody.

Following the declaration of martial law, the State Troop finally began to move into what remained of Tulsa's black neighborhoods. There, they disarmed whites and sent them home. Additional detachments of State Troops arrived from other cities throughout June 1, and the streets were eventually cleared. Businesses were ordered to close by 6:00 p.m., and all people except military or civil authorities, physicians, or relief workers were ordered off the streets by 7:00 p.m. By 8:00 p.m. on June 1, order had been restored to the city of Tulsa.

After the riots, the actions of the State Troops were largely praised by black Tulsans. Mary Parrish wrote, "Everyone with whom I met was loud in praise of the State Troops who so gallantly came to the rescue of stricken Tulsa. They used no partiality in quieting the disorder. It is the general belief that if they had reached the scene sooner, many lives and valuable property would have been saved."

**Greenwood's Legacy**

Soon after the end of the riot came the process of burying the dead. Walter White noted, "O.T. Johnson, commandant of the Tulsa Citadel of the Salvation Army, stated that on Wednesday and Thursday the Salvation Army got thirty-seven Negroes employed as grave diggers and twenty on Friday and Saturday. During the first two days these men dug 120 graves in each of which a dead Negro was buried. No coffins were used. The bodies were dumped into the holes and covered over with dirt."

The commission report found that funeral home records would confirm that black victims were buried in unmarked graves at Oaklawn Cemetery. Oral sources cited additional unmarked graves at Newblock Park, Sand Springs road, and Booker T. Washington Cemetery. According to the report, "Largely buried by strangers, there would be no headstones or graveside services for most of black Tulsa's riot dead. Nor would family members be present at the burials, as most of them were still being held under armed guard at the various detention centers. It appears that in some cases, not only did some black Tulsa families not learn how their loved ones died, but not even where they were buried."

As the dead were buried, the living returned to what remained of Greenwood, and the report discussed what they found: "What they found was a blackened landscape of vacant lots and empty streets, charred timbers and melted metal, ashes and broken dreams. Where the African-American commercial district once stood was now a ghost town of crumbling brick storefronts and the burned-out bulks of automobiles. Gone was the Dreamland and the Dixie, gone was the *Tulsa Star* and the black public library, gone was the Liberty Cafe and Elliott & Hooker's clothing store, H.L. Byars' cleaners and Mabel Little's beauty salon. Gone were literal lifetimes of sweat and hard work, and hard-won rungs on the ladder of the American Dream. Gone, too, were hundreds of homes, and more than a half-dozen African-American churches, all torched by the white invaders. Nearly ten-thousand Tulsans, practically the entire black community, was now homeless."

**A postcard of a resident standing outside his destroyed home**

News of what occurred in Tulsa spread across the country and was reported in major American newspapers. The reaction in the *New York Times* was typical of many: "The Tulsa race riot has been described as the worst outbreak of the kind in the history of the country. In some of its features it is certainly the most amazing. The attack of a young negro upon a white woman and the gathering of a small force of armed negroes do not account for the running fight for hours and the deliberate burning of the negro quarter, a square mile of buildings, including a church. The cause must lie deeper. Friction between the whites and negroes has been growing in Oklahoma. It is not altogether racial; in part it is economic. During the war Southern negroes flocked to the border State and found profitable employment. There has not been so much for them to do of late, and many of them are loafing on the streets. Not only the idle, shiftless and disorderly have worn out their welcome. It has become a common saying that 'Oklahoma is a white man's country.' When they had plenty of money to spend the negroes bought automobiles, lived high and claimed social privileges that the whites were not inclined to allow them. Drafted for service in France and praised for their patriotism, they naturally had a better opinion of themselves. All these things contributed to fan the flame of racial antagonism. The savage outburst at Tulsa leaves no room for doubt that the rough element among the whites was ripe for a rising to teach the negroes their place. Among the negroes were leaders who were ready for resistance. Unfortunately, when the explosion came the police force was found wanting and the Mayor was slow to call upon the Governor for troops. If the Tulsa collision, with its casualties and destruction of property, had occurred at Vera Cruz, the American people would have deplored the lawlessness of the Mexicans and found it shocking. It will be a bad sign if they are not made uneasy by the Oklahoma exhibition of violence and ferocity. There must be an end of that sort of thing if an approach to anarchy is to be escaped."

Governor James B.A. Robertson called for a grand jury to investigate the events surrounding the events in Tulsa. The grand jury investigation began on June 9 and continued for 12 days, with State Attorney General S. P. Freeling calling numerous witnesses. 85 individuals were indicted, and an all-white jury issued a final report.

Much to the chagrin of black Tulsans, and in the face of all evidence, the report blamed black mobs for the riot. It said in part, "We find that the recent race riot was the direct result of an effort on the part of a certain group of colored men who appeared at the courthouse on the night of May 31, 1921, for the purpose of protecting one Dick Rowland then and now in the custody of the Sheriff of Tulsa county for an alleged assault upon a young white woman. We have not been able to find any evidence either from white or colored citizens that any organized attempt was made or planned to take from the Sheriff's custody any prisoner; the crowd assembled about the courthouse being purely spectators and curiosity seekers resulting from rumors circulated about the city...There was no mob spirit among the whites, no talk of lynching and no arms. The assembly was quietly until the arrival of armed negroes, which precipitated and was the direct cause of the entire affair."

**Robertson**

The commission report seized on the miscarriage of justice, pointing out that "while a handful of African-Americans were charged with riot-related offences no white Tulsan was ever sent to prison for the murders and burnings of May 31, and June 1, 1921. In the 1920s Oklahoma courtrooms and halls of government, there would be no day of reckoning for either perpetrators or the victims of the Tulsa race riot."

In the wake of the riot, Dick Rowland, whose arrest had set the horrific chain of events into motion, had the charges against him dropped in September after the County Attorney received a letter from Sarah Page stating she did not wish to prosecute the case. According to Damie Ford, Rowland left for Kansas City, and after that, virtually nothing else is known about the rest of Rowland's life.

In much the same way, the decades following the riot saw the memory of it recede into the background. In effect, the Black Wall Street Massacre was shoved down the "memory hole," a device used in George Orwell's *1984* to censor things Big Brother decided needed to be censored. The *Tulsa Tribune* did not recognize the riot in its "Fifteen Years Ago Today" or "Twenty-five Years Ago Today" features. In 1971, the Tulsa Chamber of Commerce decided to commemorate the riot, but when they read the materials gathered by Ed Wheeler about the riot, they refused to publish any of it, and the Tulsa papers also refused to run Wheeler's story. He finally published an article in a black magazine, *Impact Magazine*; but most of Tulsa's white citizens never knew about it.

Mozella Franklin Jones, the daughter of black attorney Buck Colbert Franklin, himself a survivor of the riot, worked tirelessly to raise awareness of the riot in Tulsa and at large. Her efforts helped integrate the Tulsa Historical Society, which mounted the first ever major exhibition on the history of Tulsa's black community and created the first collection of riot photographs available to the public.

Publications about the riot slowly revived public awareness in the event. The first scholarly examination of the event was a Master's thesis written by Loren L. Gill in 1946 at the University of Tulsa. Kay M. Teall's 1971 book, *Black History in Oklahoma*, paid significant attention to the riot, as did Arthur Tolson's 1972 work, *The Black Oklahomans*. In 1975, Rudia M. Halliburton, Jr. published *The Tulsa Race War of 1921*, the first major published study of the massacre.

As the 75th anniversary of the riot neared in 1996, the Oklahoma State Legislature authorized a commission to investigate that dark chapter in state history. The commission conducted interviews and heard testimony from witnesses, and it also undertook archeological, non-invasive ground surveys of Newblock Park, Oaklawn Cemetery, and Booker T. Washington Cemetery. When the commission issued its final report, the transmittal letter said, "This Commission fully understands that it is neither judge nor jury. We have no binding legal authority to assign culpability, to determine damages, to establish a remedy, or to order either restitution or reparations. However, in our interim report in February 2000 the majority of Commissioners declared that reparations to the historic Greenwood community in real and tangible form would be good public policy and do much to repair the emotional and physical scars of this terrible incident in our shared past. We listed several recommended courses of action including direct payments to riot survivors and descendants; a scholarship fund available to students affected by the riot; establishment of an economic development enterprise zone in the historic Greenwood district; a memorial for the riot victims."

In her epilogue to the commission's final report, State Senator Maxine Horner wrote, "On June 1, 1921, Lady Justice was blind. Indeed, her eyes were gouged out. As significant, accumulation of wealth was halted and the community was again left to begin again only with its own meager resources. What is owed this community 80 years later is a repairing--education and economic incentives and something more than symbolic gestures or an official report as an apology extended to the survivors. The climate was real and official. The words of Mayor T. D. Evans spoken during the June 14, 1921 meeting of the Tulsa City Commission are brought to our attention once again: '[T]his uprising was inevitable. If that be true and this judgment had come upon us, then I say it was good generalship to let the destruction come to that section where the trouble was hatched up, put in motion and where it had its inception. All regret the wrongs that fell upon the innocent Negroes and they should receive such help as we can give them. It...is true of any warfare that the fortunes of war fall upon the innocent along with the guilty. This is true on any conflict, invasion, or uprising...Let us immediately get to the outside the fact that everything is quiet in our city, that this menace has been fully conquered, and that we are going on in a normal condition.' The mayor had his way. The conspiracy of silence was launched. We can be proud of our state for reexamining this blot on our state and our conscience, and for daring to place the light from this report on those dark days. This has been an epic journey. It can be an epic beginning. There are chapters left to write. To face, not hide again, the shame from this evil...The Oklahoma legislature is now the caretaker of this past and may disperse to the future forgiving, fair, kind, deserved and decent justice."

**Horner**

On June 1, 2001, Governor Frank Keating signed the 1921 Tulsa Race Riot Reconciliation Act into law. The bill failed to enact the commission's recommendations for reparations, but in addition to acknowledging that the event occurred and accepting the responsibility of state and local authorities in failing to prevent the violence and loss of life, the bill provided for 300 college scholarships for the descendants of Greenwood residents, economic development in Greenwood, and the creation of a memorial to those who died in the riot. In March 2001, Tulsa Mayor Kathy Taylor held a ceremony where she awarded 118 known survivors gold-plated medals with the state seal. In October 2010, the John Hope Franklin Reconciliation Park was dedicated to the memory of the victims of the riot.

**Keating**

**Taylor**

**Marc Carlson's picture of John Hope Franklin Reconciliation Park**

Anticipating the model of successful isolation played out by black entrepreneurs in places like Greenwood would have been perfectly understandable had white America been paying attention. All major black leaders, including W.E.B. Du Bois, Booker T. Washington, and Marcus Garvey, exhorted their people to build their own businesses free of white entanglement. It was a valid hope that to demonstrate self-leadership would enhance racial confidence, create trust outside the black community, and keep the black dollar in the black family where it was most needed. To do otherwise was to prolong the suffering caused by racial bias in lending, a dearth of property rights, an unwilling insurance industry, scant police protection, and little say in governmental matters. To own and self-promote was only the model, and its fulfillment required a collective of trusting black patrons who fell in with the idea that to accept lesser citizenship would leave them vulnerable in perpetuity.

The isolationist, mutually collaborative business model adopted by Greenwood was based on the idea that a neglected race should "take advantage of the disadvantage."[55] In this contrarian view of segregation, an academic version of picking up one's marbles and going home, self-rule and mutual assistance produced the desired effect. A concentration of black entrepreneurs in the Greenwood district, with strongly marked borders, exploited a strong black market, as leaders claimed it would. It mobilized a community of black purchasers to support home-grown businesses, fulfilling Booker T. Washington's dream of "an independent black economy."[56] It cemented that success by guaranteeing that no desirable product was absent. It was understood that to take away one jewelry store or beauty shop would cause the clientele to search for it elsewhere. That business being lost, the district would have risked double jeopardy, as the wayward purchaser would be introduced into a new and alien shopping district. To make the enterprise airtight, no attraction could be absent. In terms of logistics and concentration of population, Greenwood enhanced "the level of enterprise"[57] by presenting an absolute palette and eliminating the need to consider traveling outside the district. The 35 blocks centered around Greenwood and Archer, with its self-contained offering, proved that while social integration may be good for people and nations, commercial segregation is good for business in a disadvantaged collective. This has proven to be even more true in economic recessions, during which the pressure increases for being self-employed. The relative size of the ethnic population was a plus for Greenwood. For the developmental stage, the evil of "leaking money" was avoided, a financial malady in which the community dollars "wake up in the morning in the African community, but…go to sleep at night in the white community."[58] Such a strategy was referred to as the "economic detour theory,"[59] one that keeps dollars at home, important in the amassing of centralized wealth. However, it is suggested by some economic historians that clinging to this strategy eventually causes problems for collective triumph if not taken to the larger world for eventual investment. Had the infamous race riots not occurred, how long the model would have sustained itself is unclear.

For Greenwood's purposes, however, self-help was the central requirement. The isolation model had been used successfully in the past by immigrants building small businesses in one sector, such as the Italian garment industry. Equally profitable was the food industry or other collectives. They all stayed close to home and employed their neighborhood's families to keep profit from escaping. They realized that to compete as a slighted player, an economic base cannot be forged without vulnerability and frailty of fortune. For Greenwood, the lesson was well-earned and brilliantly applied, with self-help, self-production, and self-management providing the perfect "antidote"[60] to poverty. It was accomplished not through the mega-

---

[55] Robert L. Boyd, Black Enterprise in the Retail Trade During the Early 20th Century, *Sociological Focus,* Vol. 34 No. 3 (August 2001), Taylor & Francis Ltd.

[56] Robert L. Boyd

[57] Robert L. Boyd

[58] Roy L. Brooks, Integration or Separation? A Strategy for Racial Equality, Ch. 17, *Integration within the Community*, Harvard University Press

[59] Robert L. Boyd

[60] Roy L. Brooks

corporation built of outside influences, but by the family business sustained by the district's own labor force.

As for the deeper, abiding reasons for Greenwood's downfall, let loose by a trigger event, the downside of isolation may have been played out by the district's success. The lasting residue was indeed real, as black submission of patents "plunged"[61] in the following years throughout the nation. By allowing blacks to take over the business reins, the white population lost the black dependence on which it relied for financial viability, either by slaves or emancipated workers. Chris M. Messer offers four points of collective behavior in humans that make up the process of rebellion. First, people are vulnerable to destructive behavior when "confronted with an ambiguous situation."[62] Black independence certainly fulfilled that criteria. Paralleling that is the assumption that in such a setting, people look to others around them for behavioral guidance. When they see few negative consequences, they are likely to arouse more newly "emergent"[63] group norms than they might have in times of conventional circumstances. Separate from the "absolute deprivation" of minorities at a disadvantage, the white mob of Tulsa was overwhelmed with "relative deprivation" after watching yesterday's slaves wear "satin dresses and diamonds…silk shirts and gold chains."[64] Residents enjoying the good life were simultaneously aware of Tulsa's seething tension, one observing "That resentment in Tulsa was so intense."[65] White Tulsa was suddenly living a slice of the black experience, the difference being that white society had kept the majority of numbers and weaponry with which to strike back.

The Greenwood example was admirably rebuilt in large measure, but the tightness of the community was never restored. One may suggest that with increasing integration in the United States, such a guarded economy was no longer necessary. Some may differ, asserting that such a phenomenon is once again needed. John W. Rogers, the grandson of J.B. Stradford and Chairman of Aerial Investments, has carried on the tradition of supporting a black economy. He claims that among other assets, the upside of Greenwood proves that "when we are left to ourselves and don't have a knee to our neck, we can achieve extraordinary things."[66] Rogers founded the first black-owned Mutual fund company and his mother Jewel became the first African American to graduate from the School of Law at the University of Chicago. President Eisenhower appointed her as U.S. District Attorney for northern Illinois, and she was the first black woman in history to argue a case before the Supreme Court of the United States. That J.B. Stradford would have been inordinately proud of his descendant's achievements seems likely,

[61] Paul Krugman, Tulsa and the Many Sins of Racism, New York Times, June 18, 2020 – www.nytimes.com/2020/06/18/opinion/tulsa-racism.html

[62] Chris M. Messer, The Tulsa Race Riot of 1921: Toward an Integrative Theory of Collective Violence, *Journal of Social History*, Oxford University Press

[63] Chris M. Messer

[64] Meagan Day, The History of the Tulsa Massacre that Destroyed America's Wealthiest Black Neighborhood, *Timeline*, Sept. 21, 2016 – www.timeline.com/history-tulsa-face-massacre-a92bb2356a69

[65] Meagan Day

[66] Forbes

and also that he would not be in the least surprised.

Rogers laments that the Greenwood money never got its chance to be compounded over a lengthy period of time. The district's families made good use of their success, but did not accrue it with the intent to "reinvest, diversify, or expand."[67] There might have come a time in which such actions were less problematic in the modern civil rights era. In time, the black economy needed to try its wings in the larger world. However, as a result of Greenwood's destruction, perpetual generational wealth was not created in the way it might have been. He adds in response to white perceptions of the Greenwood history that all too often the white citizen does not connect bigotry to economic exploitation. They often deplore prejudice and the violence that attends it, "but have tolerated or ignored economic injustice"[68] at the same time.

In the modern era, black wealth in what was Tulsa's Greenwood District has remained "relatively flat"[69] while the white economy soars. The wealth gap in the U.S. widens, and the cultural point emphasized by the Greenwood experiment fades into a largely untaught history. In a literal sense, the "Black Wall Street" carried only a minute fraction of the volume enjoyed by the district in New York. Washington's term was always intended as a symbolic tribute, a depiction of intelligent, collaborative investment in entrepreneurship and personal drive in a race not originally thought to possess it.

Early white America, and elements of the present white culture were and continue to be in error. The model for ethnic wealth exists, and has been proven in fact over fantasy. The Greenwood experiment debunked every existing stereotype for keeping black business under heel. Such an exposure of old myths was not only important for the white business world to witness but also a demonstration of it was needed for subsequent generations of black entrepreneurs. Their professional ancestors experienced the continent's inherent cultural suppression, and had the old South's mythology lodged in their collective mindset, to be exported anywhere a black citizen might reside. Left unchallenged, the poison of surrender spread to future generations encountering more subtle tactics of the same curse. Greenwood boosted black confidence as an immovable historical fact, and handed down a model for success. The blueprint for working it is currently in the hands of any African American with the ideas and determination with which to impel its manifestation.

In the typical business model of the Greenwood District, the African American "out-whited" the white businessman. That the Greenwood District's time had not yet come is likely incorrect. Its citizens were ready, willing, and up to the task of creating a civic jewel on the prairie. More apt is that the time of fending off such a degree of resistance had not yet come. Historians to psychiatrists suggest that by the era of Greenwood's existence, the white process of acceptance

---

[67] Forbes

[68] Forbes

[69] Yahoo Finance, Why Black Wealth Has Stayed Relatively Flat Since the Tulsa Massacre - www.finance.yahoo.com/news/why-black-wwealth-has-stayed-rlatively-flat-sincetulsa-0massacre-150041181.html

had begun to run its course over far too short a time span. White sensitivities could not yet truly stand up under the pressure of possession jealousy or unfamiliar personal liberties among the slave class. Some might wonder if the time has come even in the present day for blacks to succeed without fear.

Diaries and other testimonial avenues have created interesting stories as we identify the last citizens of Greenwood still alive. Olivia Hooker, considered to be the oldest, basks in the recollection that the district "was a neighborhood where you could be treated with respect."[70] Hooker became the first black woman to join the United States Coast Guard. Her best competitor for the title is Hal Singer. On the day of Greenwood's destruction, he was hurried onto a train for Kansas City at 18 months of age. At the age of 98 in 2018, he had gone on to be a noted professional jazz saxophonist and band leader.

Of the original group of black towns created in the Oklahoma Territory, 13 exist in the present day. Most are situated in a ring around the city of Tulsa. Clearview was established in Okfuskee County, and by the second Census of the 20th century housed 48 citizens. Vernon can be found in the southwestern portion of McIntosh County, and was established four years after statehood. The population is unknown. Langston, created by Edwin McCabe, houses Langston University, and was home to 1,724 by the year of 2010. Brooksville is located in Pottawatomie County to the southwest of Tecumseh. Established somewhat earlier, it was originally named Sewell for a white doctor who owned much of the surrounding lands. Most residents departed through the early century, but the town survived, boasting 63 residents. Grayson was established in southeastern Okmulgee County barely after the turn of the century. It was named for Chief George W. Grayson and it once featured five general stores, two blacksmiths, two drug stores, a physician, and a cotton gin. At the turn of the twenty-first century, the African American percentage was 64.1%, 9.8% white and 9.8% Native American. It built two schools, two churches, and a convention center that is employed for voting. Lima was created in Seminole County two years prior and Seminoles and their freedmen blacks occupied the town. Never incorporated, the population has fallen under 270. Boley, once the most successful in the lineage leading up to Greenwood, housed many businesses including two banks, three cotton gins, and two colleges. The 2010 Census lists the population as 1,184. Tatums appeared early in the process, and was in the midst of numerous oil wells on an extensive field, in addition to a sawmill and hotel. The population is 151. Rentiesville stands only a few miles from Muskogee, home to a famous blues man and band leader, D.C. Minner. After a Civil War battle that occurred there, the town was called "the Gettysburg of the West."[71]

Among those who documented the tragedy that befell Greenwood on film, were both amateur

---

[70] NPR, Code Switch, Meet the Last Surviving Witness to the Tulsa Race Riot of 1921 – www.npr.org/section/codeswitch/2018/05/31/615546965/meet-the-last-surviving-witnesws-to-the-tulsa-race-riot-of-1921

[71] Tulsa World.com, Gallery: The 13 Historic all black towns that remain in Oklahoma, Feb. 26, 2020 – www.tulsaworld.com/news/state-and-regional/gallery-the-13-historic-all-black-touwns-that-remain-in Oklahoma/collection_7dicl7b5d-662c-54a0-a072-bc56afdf6756756.html#1

and professional documentaries that have left us visual accounts of the revival. Reverend Harold Mose Anderson, for example, was "fascinated by the movies."[72] Accordingly, he bought a home movie camera and wandered the streets of Tulsa in the years following the Second World War. The result has been *Harold Anderson's Black Wall Street Film*, with footage captured between 1948-1952 and preserved by the National Museum of American History's Archives Center. His days of roaming the avenues and residential streets of the old district documents everyday life in a resurrected Greenwood after growing up with the stories and observing the town's rebirth. As a whimsical example of old nostalgia for the original community, a board game has been created entitled *Black Wall Street*, the African American answer to *Monopoly*. The concept of the game, however, is no pure joke, but expertly teaches a young player about "both history and financial literacy."[73]

A documentary entitled *Black Wall Street* claims expanded statistics from those found in other sources. A total of 600 businesses are said to have resided within a 36 square block area, and in general, a dollar spent in Greenwood circulated over 100 times before it reached a white district. The documentary cites the number of those holding a Ph.D. who resided in the area, and a reminder that in the era of 1920s, physicians owned medical schools. The population is listed as 15,000, and of all the principles of business within the enclave, the most appreciated word was "nepotism…the one word they truly believed in."[74]

External international views have always abounded as alien systems analyze struggle for civil rights in the United States. The Marxist concept dispenses much blame for America's allegedly faulty economic system, ignoring the racial fracturing committed from the beginning, an opinion shared with much of Europe. In recounting historical reality, however, proponents of the communist system make a few salient points, such as white society's continued dependence on black labor well into the 19th century, and in certain cases, beyond. Elmer T. Allison asserts that "the foundation on which its economic, civil, and moral superstructure is built – [is] chattel slavery."[75] He adds that with the Jim Crow laws that reinserted white domination into law, the emancipation story was rendered all but fictitious, especially for the South. The plantation patriarch wanted it to remain the way it was before and after the Civil War, and he intended to have it one way or the other. He labels capitalist society as a "conspiracy against the negro,"[76] the same as any "pogrom-ridden nation against the Jews."[77] In the West, however, most simply ascribe the ongoing crisis to racism.

---

[72] Wendy Shay, contributions by Patricia Sanders, Black Wall Street on Film: A Story of Revival and Renewal, *National Museum of American History*, Feb. 24, 2017 – www.americanhistory.si.edu/blog/black-wall-street

[73] Kimberly C. Ellis, Ph.D., It's Time We All Learned About Black Wall Street and the Tulsa Massacre – dictionary.com/e/black-wall-street-tulsa-massacre

[74] Black Wall Street, Tulsa, Oklahoma, Culture, Race, and Economy – aalb.albc.com/tc/topic/1419-black-wall-street-in-tulsa-oklahoma

[75] Elmer T. Allison, The Economic Basis of the Tulsa Race Riot – www.marxisthistory.org/history/usa/parties/cpusa/192106/18-allison-tulsa-basis.pdf

[76] Elmer T. Allison

[77] Elmer T. Allison

James O. Goodwin, owner of the weekly paper, *The Oklahoma Eagle*, is connected to Greenwood through his grandfather, who worked for Smitherman's *Tulsa Star*. *The Eagle* was a long-lived paper that rose from the ashes of the *Star*, and it remained for some time in the hands of his father. When it was time, his retirement led to a summons for James to take over. When he expressed doubt due to considering other plans, his father simply said, "Come home, or I'm going to give away the paper."[78] Goodwin is quick to caution that what the black collective achieved was neither an exceptional fluke stumbled upon by an unthinking people, nor was it such a rare exception at all. Until it was brutally halted, Greenwood's quest for economic equality was accomplished in the sight of a white majority that feared it might be replicated in the future. Put simply, Black Wall Street was not operating in a strange new manner, but simply doing business the way other segments of segregated societies were doing business.

Thus, as a moniker for the historical district, America's "Black Main Street" might have been a more accurate metaphor than Washington's term, and Goodwin takes his cue from this loftier vision. He cites a higher purpose in the recognition of Greenwood's feat, one that elevates the question above racial competition, but remains all about racial equality: "The significant thing about Greenwood is that it was not just a black thing. It was quintessential America."[79]

Meanwhile, as the 100th anniversary of the massacre approaches in 2021, the city of Tulsa is still working to complete the historical record. The 2001 commission had arranged for archeological surveys of Newblock Park, Oaklawn Cemetery, and Booker T. Washington Cemetery, which witnesses had identified as possible locations for mass graves of black victims. Investigations of the sites were performed in 1997 and 1998, and preliminary data suggested there were no mass graves in these locations. Further investigations were carried out beginning in October 2019, and on December 17, 2019, the team of forensic archaeologists made an announcement that was reported in the *Washington Post*: "A team of forensic archaeologists who spent weeks using ground-penetrating radar at three sites in the city announced Monday night they found 'anomalies' consistent with mass graves that warrant further testing. The scientists said they detected the anomalies beneath the ground at Oaklawn Cemetery and an area in Tulsa called the 'The Canes,' where the Interstate 244 bridge crosses the Arkansas River. They recommended further radar survey and physical excavation of the sites. Phoebe Stubblefield, a forensic anthropologist from the University of Florida who specializes in human remains identification, called the findings promising, but also cautioned that 'we don't know what lies beneath.' Scott Hammerstedt, a scientist who worked on the geophysical survey, said at Oaklawn 'there are quite a lot of anomalies here consistent with mass graves' near a part of the cemetery where city records show 18 black people were buried in June 1921. In another section of the cemetery, they discovered 'what very much looks like a human-dug pit,' Hammerstedt said. 'This is very likely candidate to be a mass burial. We may need to investigate further.' Tulsa

---

[78] Kurtis Lee, This Newspaper Has Never Forgotten the 1921 Tulsa Race Massacre - and its Fight Continues, Workers World, LA Times – www.workers.org/1000/06/49482

[79] Antoine Gara

officials had said earlier that the next phase of the investigation could include excavation and an investigation by the State of Oklahoma's Medical Examiner's Office into causes of death. 'The cause of death determination would be an important step to the investigation,' city officials said in a statement, 'as remains will be close to 100 years old and a Spanish Influenza outbreak occurred in Tulsa in 1919 prior to the Race Massacre in 1921.' If mass graves were found, the city and oversight committee — which is made up of descendants of massacre victims, community leaders, historians and scholars — would decide on next steps, city officials said, 'as it relates to storing remains, DNA testing and genealogical research, and commemorating the grave sites and honoring the remains.' Tulsa City Councilor Vanessa Hall-Harper sat in the Carver Middle School auditorium with about 300 other people as the investigators presented their findings. She said she felt a sense of relief. 'I always knew these mass graves existed,' Hall-Harper said. 'We are pleased with the fact there is some evidence mass graves have been located. We are excited about the next steps of uncovering a cover-up and laying these bodies to rest respectfully as they should have been nearly 100 years ago.'"

As that suggests, there is still plenty of work to be done before there has been a full accounting for the worst race riot in American history.

## Online Resources

Other books about 20th century history by Charles River Editors

Other books about the Tulsa race riot on Amazon

## Bibliography

Allison, Elmer T., The Economic Basis of the Tulsa Race Riot – www.marxisthistory.org/history/usa/prties/cpusa/1921/06/18-allison-tulsa-basis

Armstrong, Thomas F., Review of Scott Ellsworth's Death in a Promised Land, the Tulsa Race Riot of 1921, Reviews in American History Vol. 11 no. 1 (March1983) Johns Hopkins University Press

Black Past, Edward P. McCabe (1850-1920) – www.blackpast.org/African American-history/maccabe-edwin-p-1850-1920/

Black Past, Deep Greenwood (Tulsa) Oklahoma (1906-) – www.blackpast.org/African American-history/deep-greenwood-tula-ok-1906/

Black Wall Street, Centennial: Tulsa Pilgrimage, 2021, The Stradfords of Black Wall Street, Tulsa – www.blackwallstrett.org/jbstradford

Black Wall Street, Tulsa, Oklahoma, Culture, Race, and Economy – www.aalbc.com/tc/topic/1419-black-wall-street-in-tulsa-oklahoma/

Bowyer, Jerry, Tulsa Massacre: The Loser Class vs. Black Entrepreneurs, Townhall Finance, June 23, 2020 – www.finance.townhall.com/columnists/jerrybowyer/2020/06/23/tulsa-massacre-the-loser-class-vs-black-entrepreneurs-n2571165

Clark, Alexis Tulsa's "Black Wall Street" Flourished as a Self-Contained Hub in Early 1900s, History.com – www.history.com/news/black-wall-street-tulsa-race-massacre

Ellis, Kimberly C., Ph.D., It's Time We All Learned About Black Wall Street and the Tulsa Massacre – www.dictionary.com/e/black-wall-street-tulsa-massacre/

Gara, Antoine, The Bezos of Black Wall Street, Forbes – www.forbes.com/peter/antoinegara/2020/06/18the-bezos-of-black-wall-street-tulsa-race-riots-1921/#5b37f7c7f321

Gilmore Glenda, Jumpin' Jim Crow: Southern Politics from Civil War to Civil Rights, Department of African American Studies, Yale University – www.afamstudies.yale.edu/publications/jumpin'-him-crow-Southern-politics-civil-war-civil-rights

Harriot, Michael, The Other Black Wall Streets, The Root – www.theroot.com, the-other-black-wall-streets-1823010812

History.com, The Trail of Tears, Feb. 21, 2020 – www.history.com/topics/native-american-history/trail-of-tears

History.com, The Red Summer of 1919 – www.history.com/black-history/chicago-race-riot0of-1919

Kirst, Sean, In Buffalo, a hero journalist in Oklahoma found new life after Tulsa massacre, Buffalo News – www.buffalonews.com/news/local/in-buffalo-a-hero-journalist-found-new-life-after-tulsa-massacre/article_a9d2b6cb-0188-50d7-bref-04245-304a9df.html

Johnson, Hannibal B., Author, Attorney, Consultant, The Ghosts of Greenwood Past, A Walk Down Black Wall Street, May 11, 2019 – www.hannibaljohnson.com/the-ghosts-of-greenwood-past-a-walk-down-black-wall-street

Krehbiel, Randy Tulsa Race Massacre, Tulsa World – www.tulsaworld.com/tulsa-race-massacre-led-by-its-determined-editor-tulsa-star-challenged-racism-and-fought-against/article_ccbf6327-422c-5160-be57-c951c237d382.html

Krugman, Paul Tulsa and the Many Sins of Racism, New York Times, June 18, 2020 – www.nytimes.com/2020/06/18/opinion/tulsa-racism.html

Lee, Kurtis, This Newspaper Has Never Forgotten the 1921 Tulsa Race Massacre – and Its Fight Continues – Workers World, LA Times, Mary 22, 2020 – www.workers.org/2000/06/49482

Lutzweiler, James, Review of Hannibal Johnson's Black Wall Street: From Riot to Renaissance in Tulsa's Historic Greenwood District, the Southwestern Historical Quarterly Vol. 103, No. 4, Texas State Historical Association

Maloney, Thomas N., University of Utah, African Americans in the 20th Century, E.H. Net – www.eh.net/encyclopedia/African Americans-in-the-20th-century

Moreno, Carlos, The Victory of Greenwood: John and Loula Williams – www.thevictoryofgreenwood.com/2020/03/15/the-victory-of-greenwood-john-and-loula-greenwood/

Oklahoma Historical Society, All-Black Town – www.oklahomahistory.org/publications/end/entry-php?entry=AL009

Oklahoma Historical Society, Greenwood District – www.okhistory.org/publications/enc/entry.php?entry=GR024

Oklahoma Historical Society, Ku Klux Klan- www.okhistory.org/publications/enc/entry.php?entry=KU001

Oklahoma Historical Society, Senate Bill One – okhistory.com/publications/enc/entry/php?entry=SE017

Roberts, Alaina E., Assistant Professor, University of Pittsburgh, Commemorating the Tulsa Massacre: A Search for Identity and Historical Complexity, June 4, 2020 – www.ncph.org/history-at-work/commemorating-tulsa-massacre/

Savage, William W. Jr., History is Clear: Alfalfa Bill Murray was a Terrible Bigot, Thursday, June 18, 2020, Non Doc.com – www.nondoc.com/2020/06/18/alfalfa-bill-murray-was-a-terrible-bigot/

Shay, Wendy, contributions by Patricia Sanders, Black Wall Street on Film: A Story of Revival and Renewal, National Museum of American History, Feb. 24, 2017 – www.americanhistory.si.edu/blog/black-wall-street

Smith, Ryan P., How Native American Slaveholders Complicate the Trail of Tears Narrative, Smithsonian Magazine –

Sean Kirst, In Buffalo, a hero journalist in Oklahoma found new life after Tulsa massacre,

Buffalo News – www.buffalonews.com/news/local/in-buffalo-a-hero-journalist-found-new-life-after-tulsa-massacre/article_a9d2b6cb-0188-50d7-bref-04245-304a9df.html

The Guardian, In 1921, A White Mob Burned Black Wall Street Down, We Still Feel That Legacy Today – www.guardian.com/commentsisfree/2020/jun/19/tulsa-1921-massacre-trump-violence-legacy/

Tulsa World.com, Gallery: The 13 Historic all black towns that remain in Oklahoma, Feb. 26, 2020 – www.tulsaworld.com/news/state-and-regional/gallery-the-13-historic-all-black-touwns-that-remain-in Oklahoma/collection_7dicl7b5d-662c-54a0-a072-bc56afdf6756756.html#1

Wills, Shomari, Origins of Black Wall Street, Investopedia, January 10, 2020 – www.investopedia.com/insights/origins-black-all-street/

Yahoo Finance, Why Black Wealth Has Stayed Relatively Flat Since the Tulsa Massacre - www.finance.yahoo.com/news/why-black-wwealth-has-stayed-rlatively-flat-sincetulsa-0massacre-150041181.html

## Free Books by Charles River Editors

We have brand new titles available for free most days of the week. To see which of our titles are currently free, click on this link.

## Discounted Books by Charles River Editors

We have titles at a discount price of just 99 cents everyday. To see which of our titles are currently 99 cents, click on this link.

Made in the USA
Las Vegas, NV
11 September 2023

77415040R00039